Current
CONTROVERSIES

| Executive Orders

Other Books in the Current Controversies Series

Executive Orders

Marcia Amidon Lusted, Book Editor

GREENHAVEN PUBLISHING

Published in 2019 by Greenhaven Publishing, LLC
353 3rd Avenue, Suite 255, New York, NY 10010

Copyright © 2019 by Greenhaven Publishing, LLC

First Edition

Articles in Greenhaven Publishing anthologies are often edited for length to meet page
requirements. In addition, original titles of these works are changed to clearly present
the main thesis and to explicitly indicate the author's opinion. Every effort is made to
ensure that Greenhaven Publishing accurately reflects the original intent of the authors.
Every effort has been made to trace the owners of the copyrighted material.

Cover image: Andrew Harrer - Pool/Getty Images

Library of Congress Cataloging-in-Publication Data

Names: Lusted, Marcia Amidon, editor.
Title: Executive orders / Marcia Amidon Lusted, book editor.
Description: New York : Greenhaven Publishing, 2019. | Series: Current
  controversies | Includes bibliographical references and index. | Audience:
  Grade 9 to 12.
Identifiers: LCCN 2017061865| ISBN 9781534503045 (library bound) | ISBN
  9781534503052 (pbk.)
Subjects: LCSH: Executive power—United States—Juvenile literature. |
  Executive orders—United States—Juvenile literature. | Presidents—United
  States—Juvenile literature.
Classification: LCC JK517 .E86 2019 | DDC 352.23/50973—dc23
LC record available at https://lccn.loc.gov/2017061865

Manufactured in the United States of America

Website: http://greenhavenpublishing.com

Contents

Chapter 1: Are Executive Orders Necessary for Presidents to Take Important Political Action?

The Heritage Foundation

Americans often hear about executive orders in media coverage of national politics, especially when the president and Congress disagree on policy. This viewpoint helps clarify what an executive order is and how it works.

Yes: Executive Orders Allow the President to Be More Effective

Vivian S. Chu and Todd Garvey

Executive orders are one vehicle of many through which the president may exercise his authority. However, an executive order—including any requirements or prohibitions—may have the force and effect of law only if the presidential action is based on the power vested in the president by the US Constitution or delegated to the president by Congress.

Lumen Learning

When a president governs alone through direct action, it may break a policy deadlock or establish new grounds for action, but it may also spark opposition that could have been handled differently through negotiation and discussion.

Leighton Walter Kille

Originally, a president's first one hundred days began not when he took the oath of office but when Congress came into session. Why then? "Because there weren't as many executive orders being delivered as you see now, and the president's success was measured by how well he got along with Congress." But with the increased use of executive orders, the first one hundred days after taking office have become an opportunity for the president to take unimpeded action.

No: Congress Should Have the Power to Check the President

While many believe the Constitution reserves the power to declare war for Congress, Joel McDurmon argues that the framers of the Constitution intentionally left the possibility for presidential declarations of war open in an effort to centralize power. However, this may give the president too much opportunity for hasty action.

Our system delegates lawmaking to Congress, implementation to the executive, and the resolution of disputes to the courts, but there is a clamor to have it otherwise. Everyone wants his or her preferred policies enacted and no one really trusts Congress with the job, so as a result constitutional order goes out the window in the service of a creative solution.

Chapter 2: Do Executive Orders Work against the Three-Branch Political System?

Certain powers are granted to the president by the Constitution, but additional powers and privileges that are not expressed in the Constitution have been acquired over time. This viewpoint looks at how the role of the president has changed over time and the different perspectives on its expanded power.

Yes: Executive Orders Violate the Separation of Powers and Can Easily Be Abused

Each new presidential administration that comes into power must build on the orders and policies left by its predecessor, which is something of which Congress needs to be mindful, regardless of which party is in control of the White House. It takes legislative action to statutorily reverse an executive or regulatory action, or it must go through the regulatory process from start to finish.

Todd Gaziano

In recent years, there has been renewed interest in the proper use and possible abuse of executive orders and other presidential directives. The increased public attention generally has been accompanied by confusion and occasional misunderstandings regarding the legality and appropriateness of various presidential actions.

No: Executive Orders Fit into the Political System

Gillian E. Metzger

All branches of the US government have a constitutional responsibility to supervise agencies and other government entities. Supervision and other systemic features of government administration—planning, policy-setting, monitoring, allocating resources, maintaining institutional structures, personnel systems, and the like—are fundamental in shaping how an agency operates and its success in meeting its statutorily imposed responsibilities.

William P. Marshall

We live in a time when political polarization is so intense that some members of one party have openly stated that they would do virtually anything to block the agenda of the sitting president. Some have even taken to opposing members of their own caucus who suggest that some compromises with the other side might be in order.

Sarah Steers and Mike Roberts

To this day, executive orders remain a powerful and immediate way for a president to advance his or her policies. However, executive orders—like other rules issued by the federal government—are subject to judicial review. Sarah Steers illustrates this by looking closely at several executive orders issued by President Obama and previous presidents.

Chapter 3: Do Executive Orders Give the President Too Much Power?

Goodwin Liu, Pamela S. Karlan, and Christopher H. Schroeder

Separating the powers of the federal government and dividing them between the House and Senate, the president, and the judiciary branch were decisions fundamental to the Constitution's design. As an "essential precaution in favor of liberty," they created a government that separates the power to make laws from the power to execute the law and further separates those powers from the power to punish individuals for violating the law.

Yes: Presidents Abuse Executive Orders

Nathan Hultman

In 2017, President Trump issued an executive order on domestic energy policy that seeks to hobble or reverse a broad set of climate and clean energy initiatives developed by the Obama administration, including an important component called the Clean Power Plan that would reduce emissions from electricity generation.

Marianne Lavelle

President Trump signed an executive order calling on every federal agency to loosen the regulatory reins on fossil fuel industries. This has been the most significant declaration of the administration's intent to retreat from action on climate change.

Todd Gaziano

Todd Gaziano argues that President Clinton abused his right to issue executive orders while in office. In addition to undoing irresponsible executive action that has already taken place, Gaziano asserts that members of Congress should also take action to limit the powers delegated to the president in order to prevent future abuses.

No: The Government Would Be at a Standstill without Executive Orders

Adam B. Cox and Cristina M. Rodríguez

On November 20, 2014, President Obama announced sweeping executive reforms of immigration law. The president's decision to defer the deportation of millions of immigrants sparked sharp debate among scholars and political figures about his authority to create such a large-scale relief program.

Union of Concerned Scientists

Thousands of bills are introduced into Congress each session, and only several hundred get signed into law. Activists have to be there at every step of the process, making sure that Congress passes strong, science-based legislation to make our world cleaner and safer, strengthen the economy, and enhance national security.

Chapter 4: Are Executive Orders Vital in Times of National Emergency?

James E. Hanley

The president is the country's chief executive, responsible for ensuring the laws are faithfully executed, managing the executive branch of the government, promoting politics through legislation and rulemaking, and representing the US in international relations.

Yes: When a Quick Response Is Necessary, Executive Orders Give the President the Power to Act

Alison Kodjak

Opioid abuse is a crisis, but is it an emergency? That's the question gripping Washington after President Trump's Commission on Combating Drug Addiction and the Opioid Crisis recommended that the president declare the epidemic a national emergency. Alison Kodjak makes the argument that doing so would allow for a more effective response to the opioid crisis and lists the ways in which the government could act.

Jeanne Mirer and Marjorie Cohn

On May 6, 1935, with the country in the midst of the Great Depression and with indirect efforts to create jobs proving unsuccessful at reducing unemployment rates, President Franklin D. Roosevelt signed Executive Order 7034 and appropriated $4.8 billion for the Works Progress Administration (WPA).

No: Executive Orders Are Too Easily Misused and Overturned to Be Useful

Environmental Law Institute

All presidential administrations employ a wide variety of executive orders and other executive actions that serve important organizational, symbolic, and policy purposes. Especially in times of political gridlock, the idea of making sweeping changes "with the stroke of a pen" can be appealing, but it is equally easy for the successor's administration to alter or reverse these policies. Such changes routinely occur with a change of parties.

Brandon Schmuck

A number of Americans are questioning the lack of limits on authority that has been granted to presidents through executive orders. This fear is justifiable, as the idea of any individual having the power to make such orders is both frightening and a risk to the welfare of this nation.

Foreword

"Controversy" is a word that has an undeniably unpleasant connotation. It carries a definite negative charge. Controversy can spoil family gatherings, spread a chill around classroom and campus discussion, inflame public discourse, open raw civic wounds, and lead to the ouster of public officials. We often feel that controversy is almost akin to bad manners, a rude and shocking eruption of that which must not be spoken or thought of in polite, tightly guarded society. To avoid controversy, to quell controversy, is often seen as a public good, a victory for etiquette, perhaps even a moral or ethical imperative.

Yet the studious, deliberate avoidance of controversy is also a whitewashing, a denial, a death threat to democracy. It is a false sterilizing and sanitizing and superficial ordering of the messy, ragged, chaotic, at times ugly processes by which a healthy democracy identifies and confronts challenges, engages in passionate debate about appropriate approaches and solutions, and arrives at something like a consensus and a broadly accepted and supported way forward. Controversy is the megaphone, the speaker's corner, the public square through which the citizenry finds and uses its voice. Controversy is the life's blood of our democracy and absolutely essential to the vibrant health of our society.

Our present age is certainly no stranger to controversy. We are consumed by fierce debates about technology, privacy, political correctness, poverty, violence, crime and policing, guns, immigration, civil and human rights, terrorism, militarism, environmental protection, and gender and racial equality. Loudly competing voices are raised every day, shouting opposing opinions, putting forth competing agendas, and summoning starkly different visions of a utopian or dystopian future. Often these voices attempt to shout the others down; there is precious little listening and considering among the cacophonous din. Yet listening and considering, too, are essential to the health of a democracy. If controversy is democracy's lusty lifeblood, respectful listening and careful thought are its higher faculties, its brain, its conscience.

Current Controversies does not shy away from or attempt to hush the loudly competing voices. It seeks to provide readers with as wide and representative as possible a range of articulate voices on any given controversy of the day, separates each one out to allow it to be heard clearly and fairly, and encourages careful listening to each of these well-crafted, thoughtfully expressed opinions, supplied by some of today's leading academics, thinkers, analysts, politicians, policy makers, economists, activists, change agents, and advocates. Only after listening to a wide range of opinions on an issue, evaluating the strengths and weaknesses of each argument, assessing how well the facts and available evidence mesh with the stated opinions and conclusions, and thoughtfully and critically examining one's own beliefs and conscience can the reader begin to arrive at his or her own conclusions and articulate his or her own stance on the spotlighted controversy.

This process is facilitated and supported in each Current Controversies volume by an introduction and chapter overviews that provide readers with the essential context they need to begin engaging with the spotlighted controversies, with the debates surrounding them, and with their own perhaps shifting or nascent opinions on them. Chapters are organized around several key questions that are answered with diverse opinions representing all points on the political spectrum. In its content, organization, and methodology, readers are encouraged to determine the authors' points of view and purpose, interrogate and analyze the various arguments and their rhetoric and structure, evaluate the arguments' strengths and weaknesses, test their claims against available facts and evidence, judge the validity of the reasoning, and bring into clearer, sharper focus the reader's own beliefs and conclusions and how they may differ from or align with those in the collection or those of classmates.

Research has shown that reading comprehension skills improve dramatically when students are provided with compelling, intriguing, and relevant "discussable" texts. The subject matter of these collections could not be more compelling, intriguing, or urgently relevant to today's students and the world they are poised to inherit. The anthologized articles also provide the basis for stimulating, lively, and passionate classroom debates. Students who are compelled to anticipate objections to their own argument and identify the flaws in those of an opponent read more carefully, think more critically, and steep themselves in relevant context, facts, and information more thoroughly. In short, using discussable text of the kind provided by every single volume in the Current Controversies series encourages close reading, facilitates reading comprehension, fosters research, strengthens critical thinking, and greatly enlivens and energizes classroom discussion and participation. The entire learning process is deepened, extended, and strengthened.

If we are to foster a knowledgeable, responsible, active, and engaged citizenry, we must provide readers with the intellectual, interpretive, and critical-thinking tools and experience necessary to make sense of the world around them and of the all-important debates and arguments that inform it. We must encourage them not to run away from or attempt to quell controversy but to embrace it in a responsible, conscientious, and thoughtful way, to sharpen and strengthen their own informed opinions by listening to and critically analyzing those of others. This series encourages respectful engagement with and analysis of current controversies and competing opinions and fosters a resulting increase in the strength and rigor of one's own opinions and stances. As such, it helps readers assume their rightful place in the public square and provides them with the skills necessary to uphold their awesome responsibility—guaranteeing the continued and future health of a vital, vibrant, and free democracy.

Introduction

> *We're not just going to be waiting for legislation in order to make sure that we're providing Americans the kind of help they need. I've got a pen and I've got a phone.*
>
> —*Barack Obama*

President Donald Trump, the 45th president of the United States, was inaugurated on January 20, 2017. During his first 100 days in office in 2017, President Trump signed 32 executive orders. By the end of 2017, President Trump had signed 55 executive orders, and was on track to have issued more orders than any president since World War II. These orders included some that were fairly inconsequential for most Americans, such as authorizing the revision of an official seal for the National Credit Union. However, others had both immediate and potentially long-lasting results, such as suspending the entry of immigrants from seven Muslim majority countries—Syria, Iran, Iraq, Libya, Sudan, Yemen, and Somalia—as well as an order to reorganize and reduce government agencies and an order making it easier for infrastructure projects to get past environmental reviews. There were also orders intended to dismantle President Obama's Affordable Care Act, orders intended to help combat the opioid drug crisis, orders promoting the purchase of American goods and the hiring American workers, and an order increasing border patrol and immigration regulation and facilitating the construction of a border wall with Mexico. Many of President Trump's executive orders were intended to suggest immediate action in fulfilling some of his campaign promises.[1]

Executive orders are not new, and many presidents have made frequent use of them to further legislation that they felt was of great importance. In his eight years in office, President Barack Obama signed 276 executive orders, and President Bill Clinton signed 305 orders in seven years. The orders that President Trump signed in 2017 alone frequently dealt with controversial subjects, and some Americans became concerned about the potential for these orders to have negative effects on the country and its people. For this reason, many Americans began seeking clarification and information about what executive orders involve, how they are created and enacted, and whether they make permanent changes to the US government and its policies.

So what exactly is an executive order? It is an official instruction or directive that comes directly from a president or governor (the head of the executive branch of a national or state government, respectively) without any input, discussion, or approval from the legislative or judicial branches. Executive orders can only be issued in regard to federal or state agencies, not to individual citizens. However, citizens are often directly affected by executive orders. President George Washington issued the very first executive order on April 22, 1793. The order instructed federal officers to prosecute any citizen who interfered in the war between England and France. Washington chose to use an executive order for this because Congress was not in session at the time.[2] Since this first executive order, a number of famous and infamous presidential actions have taken place through their use. President Theodore Roosevelt used an executive order to protect 130 million acres of land and establish five national parks. President Franklin Roosevelt used an executive order to create internment camps during World War II, and President Ford used one to pardon President Richard Nixon in 1974 following the Watergate scandal. Though presidents often used these orders at times when quick action was necessary and Congress was not available, other presidents realized that it was a way to enact their priorities for policies, especially if Congress was hostile to their ideas. Paul Begala, an aide to President Bill

Clinton, phrased it, "Stroke of the pen, law of the land. Kind of cool." As President Obama said, "We can't wait for Congress to do its job. So where they won't act, I will."[3]

Executive orders allow the power of the president and the executive branch of government to expand, but they are also controversial for this reason. The president does not automatically create a new law or authorize the funding for one of his executive orders, but he can push through policy changes without having to go through Congress. And if his order has a basis in laws already passed by Congress or falls under the powers given to the president as head of state, head of the executive branch, and commander in chief of the nation's armed forces, then according to the Constitution, it has the force of a law. However, there are checks and balances to executive orders. They are subject to legal review, and the Supreme Court or lower federal courts can cancel an executive order if it determines that it is unconstitutional, which occurred with several versions of President Trump's immigration orders. Congress can also revoke an executive order with new legislation.

Because of President Trump's enthusiasm for using executive orders to enable quick action, Americans are now more aware of them than they may have been during previous presidencies. Some people find them to be an effective way for the president to fulfill his campaign promises when Congress is divided or uncooperative. Others find them a dangerous tool that allows possibly catastrophic changes to be made to the country's policies. It is this controversy that will be explored through the opposing viewpoints found in *Current Controversies: Executive Orders.*

Notes

1. "Executive orders," Federal register, National Archives and Records Administration. Accessed December 27, 2017. https://www.federalregister.gov/executive-orders

2. Dave Roos, "How Executive Orders Work." How Stuff Works. Accessed December 27, 2017. https://people.howstuffworks.com/executive-order.htm

3. Richard Wolf, "Obama uses executive powers to get past Congress." *USA Today*, October 27, 2011. https://usatoday30.usatoday.com/news/washington/story/2011-10-26/obama-executive-orders/50942170/1

Current
CONTROVERSIES

Are Executive Orders Necessary for Presidents to Take Important Political Action?

What Are Executive Orders?

The Heritage Foundation

The mission of the Heritage Foundation is to formulate and promote conservative public policies based on the principles of free enterprise, limited government, individual freedom, traditional American values, and a strong national defense.

Americans often hear about executive orders in media coverage of national politics these days, especially when the president and Congress disagree on policy.

But what exactly is an executive order?

And why was it such a big deal, for example, that President Barack Obama moved to protect millions of illegal immigrants from deportation using his executive powers?

Put simply, an executive order is a type of written instruction that presidents use to work their will through the executive branch of government.

From George Washington on, our presidents have issued many forms of directives, the most familiar being executive orders and two others: Presidential memoranda and presidential proclamations. (One proclamation by Abraham Lincoln in 1863, students are taught in school with some oversimplification, "freed the slaves.")

Each of these forms may direct the actions of government officials and agencies, and possibly affect the legal rights and responsibilities of private parties.

The main difference between them is that federal law requires, with few exceptions, executive orders and proclamations "of general applicability and Legal effect" to be published in the Federal Register, where federal regulations are published. Other directives may be published or not, at the president's discretion.

"Executive Orders," Heritage Foundation. Reprinted by permission.

Presidential Authority

Under our system of government, the president's authority to issue such orders (or to engage in any other form of unilateral executive action) must come from the Constitution or federal law. Put another way, an executive order can be used to execute a power the commander in chief already has. It can't be used to give the presidency new powers.

In particular, Article II of the Constitution assigns the president the roles of commander in chief, head of state, chief law enforcement officer, and head of the executive branch. The president has the sole constitutional obligation to "take care that the laws be faithfully executed," and is granted broad discretion over federal law enforcement decisions.

"He has not only the power, but also the responsibility to see that the Constitution and laws are interpreted correctly," Heritage Foundation scholar Todd Gaziano wrote in 2001.

When the president lawfully exercises one of these responsibilities, scholars generally agree, the scope of his authority to issue executive orders and other directives is especially broad. As such, Congress has little ability to regulate or limit that authority.

When a president's authority comes from power granted by statute, Congress is free to negate or modify that authority, or pass legislation to nullify the order itself, because the Constitution empowers Congress to make the laws that govern us. Still, the president has to sign the law enacting that change, unless Congress is able to override his veto.

Federal courts also may strike down executive orders that exceed the scope of the president's authority, as an appeals court did with President Bill Clinton's order forbidding government contracts with businesses that employed strike-breakers, and the Supreme Court did with his order requiring the government to use foreign languages in providing federal benefits and services.

A Short History

Washington and his successors as president have issued thousands of executive orders. The State Department began numbering them in 1907, working from files going back to 1862. The Federal Register Act of 1936 built on that effort. Today, the official number is close to 14,000.

Even so, approximately 1,500 unnumbered executive orders also have been compiled, according to the American Presidency Project, which notes that there may be as many as 50,000 unnumbered orders.

Washington issued a total of eight executive orders in his two terms, according to the project's data, while John Adams, James Madison, and James Monroe all issued only one. Presidents who issued the least also include Thomas Jefferson (four) and John Quincy Adams (three).

Lincoln, with 48 executive orders, was the first to approach 50. Ulysses Grant with 217 was the first to break 200, and he held that record until Theodore Roosevelt came along (1,081). Other leading issuers of executive orders include Woodrow Wilson (1,803), Calvin Coolidge (1,203), Herbert Hoover (968), and Harry Truman (907).

The record holder by far, though, is Franklin Roosevelt with 3,721—five of which the Supreme Court overturned in 1935. Other modern presidents and their tallies include Dwight Eisenhower (484), Lyndon Johnson (325), Richard Nixon (346), Jimmy Carter (320), Ronald Reagan (381), George H.W. Bush (166), Bill Clinton (364), George W. Bush (291), and Barack Obama (260 as of Nov. 20).

Congressional Latitude

Scholars say Congress has some latitude in defining the procedures the president must follow to exercise executive authority. Even so, the Constitution imposes some limits on the lawmakers' ability to micromanage the president's decision-making and enforcement of laws.

The constitutional separation of powers among the executive, legislative, and judicial branches not only supports but limits a president's authority to issue executive orders and other directives. So some friction naturally occurs.

It's important to consider that the measure of abuse of this presidential authority isn't the total number of directives, but whether any were illegal or improper.

While Reagan and both Bushes—all Republican presidents—issued significant numbers of executive orders, conservative scholars argue that Democrats Clinton and Obama routinely overstepped their authority to issue such directives in arenas where Congress had not acted.

"Because few reforms can be imposed on a president over his veto," Gaziano wrote in 2001 as Bush took over from Clinton, "it makes sense for Congress to work with the new president on such reforms rather than overreact to the abuses of the last president."

Overuse and Abuse of Executive Power

During the Obama presidency, Congress frequently clashed with the executive branch on his use of executive orders and other unilateral actions that he undertook. Obama, however, isn't the first president to face a backlash.

Some of the more controversial executive orders or actions of the modern presidency include:

- 1933, Roosevelt: Franklin Roosevelt's orders forbidding the hoarding of gold during the Depression and, during World War II, giving the military authority to confine Japanese and German Americans to guarded camps.
- 1948, Truman: Truman's 1948 order racially integrating the armed forces, and his 1952 order putting all steel mills under federal control.
- 1957, Eisenhower: Eisenhower's order desegregating public schools.
- 1961, Kennedy: John F. Kennedy's order requiring

government contractors to "take affirmative action" to hire and treat employees without regard to "race, creed, color, or national origin."

- 1996, Clinton: Clinton's multiple orders allowing preferential treatment in federal contracting based on race or ethnicity in 2000, and authorizing the government to take private land under the Antiquities Act of 1906 (including his 1996 designation of 1.7 million acres in Utah as a national monument).

- 2001, George W. Bush: George W. Bush's 2001 order restricting public access to the papers of former presidents, and his 2008 order directing federal agencies to ignore future budget earmarks that lawmakers don't vote on and include in legislation that passes.

What a New President Can Do

In the case of Obama's action granting amnesty to illegal immigrants and allowing them to apply for work permits, states asked the federal courts to step in and halt this executive amnesty. And they did so, at least temporarily, pending future rulings on whether those actions were constitutional and should be permanently enjoined.

Conservatives argued that Obama used executive orders to achieve results he failed to get through Congress, not only on immigration but on issues such as health care, gun control, cybersecurity, energy, the environment, education, and gender identity, among others.

As the 45th president, Republican Donald Trump will have the opportunity to review, revise, or revoke Obama's executive orders —just as the younger Bush did in regard to Clinton's directives, and Obama did in regard to Bush's.

In its Blueprint for a New Administration, The Heritage Foundation recommends that Trump rescind specific executive orders and other directives from Obama, including those mandating global warming and green energy practices for federal agencies;

waiving work requirements for welfare recipients; restricting enforcement of immigration laws; allowing union dues to be used for political activities or lobbying; and requiring "dignity and respect" for individuals in collecting intelligence on foreign threats.

Executive Orders Are One Way for the President to Exercise Authority

Vivian S. Chu and Todd Garvey

Vivian S. Chu and Todd Garvey are both legislative attorneys with the Congressional Research Service, providing nonpartisan legal analysis to Congress.

Executive orders are one vehicle of many through which the President may exercise his authority. While the President's ability to use executive orders as a means of implementing presidential power has been established as a matter of law and practice, it is equally well established that the substance of an executive order, including any requirements or prohibitions, may have the force and effect of law only if the presidential action is based on power vested in the President by the US Constitution or delegated to the President by Congress. The President's authority to issue executive orders does not include a grant of power to implement policy decisions that are not otherwise authorized by law. Indeed, an executive order that implements a policy in direct contradiction to the law will be without legal effect unless the order can be justified as an exercise of the President's exclusive and independent constitutional authority.

This report first reviews the "definition" of an executive order and how it is distinguishable from other written instruments, and then provides an overview of the President's constitutional authority to issue such directives. Next, the report discusses the legal framework relied on by the courts to analyze the validity of presidential actions, and also discusses the roles of the President and Congress in modifying and revoking executive orders.

"Executive Orders: Issuance, Modification, and Revocation," by Vivian S. Chu and Todd Garvey, Congressional Research Service, April 16, 2014.

Definition and Authority

Presidents have historically utilized various written instruments to direct the executive branch and implement policy. These include executive orders, presidential memoranda, and presidential proclamations. The definitions of these instruments, including the differences between them, are not easily discernible, as the US Constitution does not contain any provision referring to these terms or the manner in which the President may communicate directives to the executive branch. A widely accepted description of executive orders and proclamations comes from a report issued in 1957 by the House Government Operations Committee:

> Executive orders and proclamations are directives or actions by the President. When they are founded on the authority of the President derived from the Constitution or statute, they may have the force and effect of law.... In the narrower sense Executive orders and proclamations are written documents denominated as such.... Executive orders are generally directed to, and govern actions by, Government officials and agencies. They usually affect private individuals only indirectly. Proclamations in most instances affect primarily the activities of private individuals. Since the President has no power or authority over individual citizens and their rights except where he is granted such power and authority by a provision in the Constitution or by statute, the President's proclamations are not legally binding and are at best hortatory unless based on such grants of authority.

The distinction between these instruments—executive orders, presidential memoranda, and proclamations—seems to be more a matter of form than of substance, given that all three may be employed to direct and govern the actions of government officials and agencies. Moreover, if issued under a legitimate claim of authority and made public, a presidential directive could have the force and effect of law, "of which all courts are bound to take notice, and to which all courts are bound to give effect." The only technical difference is that executive orders must be published in the *Federal Register*, while presidential memoranda and proclamations are published only when the President determines that they have "general applicability and legal effect."

Just as there is no definition of executive orders, presidential memoranda, and proclamations in the US Constitution, there is, likewise, no specific provision authorizing their issuance. As such, authority for the execution and implementation of these written instruments stems from implied constitutional and statutory authority. In the constitutional context, presidential power is derived from Article II of the US Constitution, which states that "the executive power shall be vested in a President of the United States," that "the President shall be Commander in Chief of the Army and Navy of the United States," and that the President "shall take Care that the Laws be faithfully executed." The President's power to issue these directives may also derive from express or implied statutory authority.

Despite the amorphous nature of the authority to issue executive orders, presidential memoranda, and proclamations, these instruments have been employed by every President since the inception of the Republic. Notably, executive orders historically have been more contentious as Presidents have issued them over a wide range of controversial areas such as the establishment of internment camps during World War II; the suspension of the writ of habeas corpus; and equal treatment in the armed services without regard to race, color, religion, or national origin. However, Presidents have also used executive orders for arguably more mundane governing tasks such as directing federal agencies to evaluate their ability to streamline customer service delivery and establishing advisory committees. Because there is no underlying constitutional or statutory authority that dictates the circumstances under which the President must issue an executive order, it is probable that the President also could have chosen to issue presidential memoranda rather than executive orders. As a matter or historical practice, however, it seems that Presidents are more apt to utilize executive orders on matters that may benefit from public awareness or be subject to heightened scrutiny. Memoranda, on the other hand, are often used to carry out routine executive decisions and determinations, or to direct agencies to perform duties consistent with the law or implement laws that are presidential priorities.

Judicially Enforced Limitations

Presidents' broad usage of executive orders to effectuate policy goals has led some Members of Congress and various legal commentators to suggest that many such orders constitute unilateral executive lawmaking that impacts the interests of private citizens and encroaches upon congressional power. The Supreme Court in *Youngstown Sheet & Tube Co. v. Sawyer* established the framework for analyzing whether the President's issuance of an executive order is a valid presidential action. As discussed below, the framework established by Justice Robert H. Jackson in his concurring opinion has become more influential than the majority opinion authored by Justice Hugo Black, and has since been employed by the courts to analyze the validity of controversial presidential actions.

Youngstown Sheet & Tube Co. v. Sawyer

In 1952, President Harry S. Truman, in an effort to avert the effects of a workers' strike during the Korean War, issued an executive order directing the Secretary of Commerce to take possession of most of the nation's steel mills to ensure continued production. This order, challenged by the steel companies, was declared unconstitutional by the Supreme Court in *Youngstown*. Justice Black, writing for the majority, stated that under the Constitution, "the President's power to see that laws are faithfully executed refuted the idea that he is to be a lawmaker." Specifically, Justice Black maintained that presidential authority to issue such an executive order, "if any, must stem either from an act of Congress or from the Constitution itself." Applying this reasoning, the Court concluded the President's executive order was effectively a legislative act because no statute or constitutional provision authorized such presidential action. The Court further noted that Congress rejected seizure as a means of settling labor disputes during consideration of the Taft-Hartley Act of 1947, and instead adopted other processes. Given this characterization, the Court deemed the executive order to be an unconstitutional violation of the separation-of-powers doctrine, explaining that "the Founders of this Nation entrusted the lawmaking power to the Congress alone in both good and bad times."

While Justice Black's majority opinion in *Youngstown* seems to refute the notion that the President possesses implied constitutional powers, it is important to note that there were five concurrences in the decision, four of which maintained that implied presidential authority adheres in certain contexts. Of these concurrences, Justice Jackson's has proven to be the most influential, even surpassing the impact of Justice Black's majority opinion. Jackson's concurrence, as discussed below, is based on the proposition that presidential powers may be influenced by congressional action.

Justice Jackson's Concurrence in Youngstown

In his concurring opinion, Justice Jackson established a tripartite scheme for analyzing the validity of presidential actions in relation to constitutional and congressional authority. Because "[p]residential powers are not fixed but fluctuate, depending upon their disjunction or conjunction with those of Congress," Justice Jackson acknowledged that the three categories he established were a "somewhat over-simplified grouping," but they nonetheless assist in identifying "practical situations in which a President may doubt, or others may challenge, his powers, and by distinguishing roughly the legal consequences of this factor of relativity."

Under the tripartite scheme, the President's authority to act is considered at a maximum when he acts pursuant to an express or implied authorization of Congress because this includes "all that he possesses in his own right plus all that Congress can delegate." Such action "would be supported by the strongest of presumptions and the widest latitude of judicial interpretation."

However, where Congress has neither granted nor denied authority to the President, Justice Jackson maintained that the President could still act upon his own independent powers. For this second category, there is a "zone of twilight in which [the President] and Congress may have concurrent authority, or in which distribution is uncertain." Under these circumstances, Justice Jackson observed that congressional acquiescence or silence "may sometimes, at least as a practical matter, enable, if not invite, measures on independent presidential responsibility," yet "any actual test of power is likely to depend on the imperatives of events and contemporary imponderables rather than on abstract theories of law."

In contrast, the President's authority is considered at its "lowest ebb" when he "takes measures incompatible with the express or implied will of Congress ... for he can only rely upon his own constitutional powers minus any constitutional powers of Congress over the matter." Justice Jackson observed that courts generally "sustain exclusive presidential control ... only by disabling the Congress from acting upon the subject." He cautioned that examination of presidential action under this third category deserved more scrutiny because for the President to exercise such "conclusive and preclusive" power would endanger "the equilibrium established by our constitutional system."

Applying this framework to President Truman's action, Justice Jackson determined that analysis under the first category was inappropriate, due to the fact that seizure of the steel mills had not been authorized by Congress, either implicitly or explicitly. Justice Jackson also determined that the President Truman's action could not be defended under the second category because Congress had addressed the issue of seizure through statutory policies that conflicted with the President's action. Justice Jackson concluded that the President's action could be sustained only if it passed muster under the third category, that is, by finding "that seizure of such strike-bound industries is within his domain and beyond the control of Congress." Specifically, the President would have to rely on "any remainder of executive power after such powers as Congress may have over the subject" to lawfully seize steel mills. Given that the seizure of steel mills was within the scope of congressional power, the exercise of presidential power under these circumstances was "most vulnerable to attack and [left the President] in the least favorable of possible constitutional postures."

Justice Jackson's framework for analyzing the validity of presidential actions has endured into the modern era. For example, the Supreme Court in *Dames & Moore v. Regan* referenced Justice Jackson's analytical framework when it upheld executive orders and agency regulations that nullified all non-Iranian interests in Iranian assets and suspended all settlement claims. Because the President had been delegated broad authority under the International Emergency Economic Powers Act to nullify non-Iranian interests, the Court, invoking Justice Jackson's first category, stated that such action "is supported by the strongest presumption and the widest latitude of judicial interpretation." With respect to the suspension of claims, the Court upheld the President's action on the basis that Congress had enacted legislation in the area of the President's authority to deal with international crises and had "implicitly approved the longstanding practice of claims settlements by executive agreement."

However, not all courts necessarily invoke Justice Jackson's tripartite framework in evaluating executive orders and actions. For instance, in 1995 the US Court of Appeals for the District of Columbia Circuit (D.C. Circuit) in *Chamber of Commerce v. Reich* overturned an executive order issued by President William J. Clinton by using traditional tools of statutory interpretation. Relying on his authority pursuant to the Federal Property and Administrative Services Act (FPASA), President Clinton issued Executive Order 12954, which directed the Secretary of Labor to adopt such rules and orders as necessary to ensure that federal agencies would not contract with employers that permanently replaced striking employees. The D.C. Circuit in Reich did not invoke or refer to the *Youngstown* decision when reviewing the validity of the executive order. The court nonetheless determined that President Clinton's executive order, although issued pursuant to broad authority delegated to him under FPASA, was invalid and without legal effect because it conflicted with a provision of the National Labor Relations Act, which guarantees the right to hire permanent replacements during strikes.

Presidential Revocation and Modification of Executive Orders

Executive orders are undoubtedly one of many tools available to Presidents to further policy goals during his Administration. By their very nature, however, executive orders lack stability, especially in the face of evolving presidential priorities. The President is free to revoke, modify, or supersede his own orders or those issued by a predecessor.

The practice of Presidents modifying and revoking executive orders is exemplified particularly where orders have been issued to assert control over and influence the agency rulemaking process. Beginning with President Gerald Ford's Administration, the following timeline demonstrates the gradual modification by succeeding Presidents in supplementing the congressionally mandated rulemaking process with a uniform set of standards regarding cost-benefit considerations.

- President Gerald Ford issued Executive Order 11821, which required agencies to issue inflation impact statements for proposed regulations.
- President Jimmy Carter altered this practice with Executive Order 12044, which required agencies to consider the potential economic impact of certain rules and identify potential alternatives.
- President Ronald Reagan revoked President Carter's order and implemented a scheme that arguably asserted much more extensive control over the rulemaking process. He issued Executive Order 12291, which directed agencies to implement rules only if the "potential benefits to society for

the regulation outweigh the potential costs to society." This required agencies to prepare a cost-benefit analysis for any proposed rule that could have a significant economic impact.

- President William J. Clinton later issued Executive Order 12866, which modified the system established during the Reagan Administration. While retaining many of the basic features of President Reagan's order, Executive Order 12866 arguably eased cost-benefit analysis requirements, and recognized the primary duty of agencies to fulfill the duties committed to them by Congress.

- President George W. Bush subsequently issued two executive orders—Executive Orders 13258 and 13422—both of which amended the Clinton executive order Executive Order 13258 concerned regulatory planning and review, and it removed references from Clinton's executive order regarding the role of the Vice President, and instead referenced the Director of the Office of Management and Budget (OMB) or the Chief of Staff to the President. Executive Order 13422 defined guidance documents and significant guidance documents and applied several parts of the Clinton executive order to guidance documents. It also required each agency head to designate a presidential appointee to the newly created position of regulatory policy officer. Executive Order 13422 also made changes to the Office of Information and Regulatory Affairs' (OIRA) duties and authorities, including a requirement that OIRA be given advance notice of significant guidance documents.

President Barack Obama revoked both of these orders via Executive Order 13497. This order also instructed the Director of OMB and the heads of executive departments and agencies to rescind orders, rules, guidelines, and policies that implemented President Bush's executive orders. In addition, President Obama issued two other executive orders on the regulatory review process. The first, Executive Order 13563, reaffirmed and supplemented the principles of regulatory review in Executive Order 12866. Obama's order addressed public participation and agency coordination in simplifying and harmonizing regulations for industries with significant regulatory requirements. The order also instructed agencies to consider flexible approaches to regulation, required them to ensure the objectivity of scientific and technical information and processes that support regulations, and mandated that agencies develop a preliminary plan to review existing significant regulations for potential modifications or repeal. The second executive order, Executive Order 13579, stated that independent regulatory agencies should also comply "to the extent permitted by law" with the goals and requirements of the first order, Executive Order 13563.

[...]

Letting Presidents Take Direct Action

Lumen Learning

Lumen Learning's mission is to make learning opportunities available to all students, regardless of socioeconomic background, by using open educational resources (OER) to create well-designed and low-cost course materials that replace expensive textbooks.

A president's powers can be divided into two categories: direct actions the chief executive can take by employing the formal institutional powers of the office and informal powers of persuasion and negotiation essential to working with the legislative branch. When a president governs alone through direct action, it may break a policy deadlock or establish new grounds for action, but it may also spark opposition that might have been handled differently through negotiation and discussion. Moreover, such decisions are subject to court challenge, legislative reversal, or revocation by a successor. What may seem to be a sign of strength is often more properly understood as independent action undertaken in the wake of a failure to achieve a solution through the legislative process, or an admission that such an effort would prove futile. When it comes to national security, international negotiations, or war, the president has many more opportunities to act directly and in some cases must do so when circumstances require quick and decisive action.

Domestic Policy

The president may not be able to appoint key members of his or her administration without Senate confirmation, but he or she can demand the resignation or removal of cabinet officers, high-ranking appointees (such as ambassadors), and members of

"Presidential Governance: Direct Presidential Action," Lumen Learning. https://courses.lumenlearning.com/amgovernment/chapter/presidential-governance-direct-presidential-action/. Licensed under CC by 4.0 International.

the presidential staff. During Reconstruction, Congress tried to curtail the president's removal power with the Tenure of Office Act (1867), which required Senate concurrence to remove presidential nominees who took office upon Senate confirmation. Andrew Johnson's violation of that legislation provided the grounds for his impeachment in 1868. Subsequent presidents secured modifications of the legislation before the Supreme Court ruled in 1926 that the Senate had no right to impair the president's removal power.[1] In the case of Senate failure to approve presidential nominations, the president is empowered to issue recess appointments (made while the Senate is in recess) that continue in force until the end of the next session of the Senate (unless the Senate confirms the nominee).

The president also exercises the power of pardon without conditions. Once used fairly sparingly—apart from Andrew Johnson's wholesale pardons of former Confederates during the Reconstruction period—the pardon power has become more visible in recent decades. President Harry S. Truman issued over two thousand pardons and commutations, more than any other post–World War II president. President Gerald Ford has the unenviable reputation of being the only president to pardon another president (his predecessor Richard Nixon, who resigned after the Watergate scandal). While not as generous as Truman, President Jimmy Carter also issued a great number of pardons, including several for draft dodging during the Vietnam War. President Reagan was reluctant to use the pardon as much, as was President George H. W. Bush. President Clinton pardoned few people for much of his presidency, but did make several last-minute pardons, which led to some controversy. To date, Barack Obama has seldom used his power to pardon.

Presidents may choose to issue executive orders or proclamations to achieve policy goals. Usually, executive orders direct government agencies to pursue a certain course in the absence of congressional action. A more subtle version pioneered by recent presidents is the executive memorandum, which tends to attract less attention. Many of the most famous executive orders have come in times of war or invoke the president's authority as commander-in-chief, including Franklin Roosevelt's order permitting the internment of Japanese Americans in 1942 and Harry Truman's directive desegregating the armed forces (1948). The most famous presidential proclamation was Abraham Lincoln's Emancipation Proclamation (1863), which declared slaves in areas under Confederate control to be free (with a few exceptions).

Executive orders are subject to court rulings or changes in policy enacted by Congress. During the Korean War, the Supreme Court revoked Truman's order seizing the steel industry. These orders are also subject to reversal by presidents who come after, and recent presidents have wasted little time reversing the orders of their predecessors in cases of disagreement. Sustained executive orders, which are those not overturned in courts, typically have some prior authority from Congress that legitimizes them. When there is no prior authority, it is much more likely that an executive order will be overturned by a later president. For this reason, this tool has become less common in recent decades.

Finally, presidents have also used the line-item veto and signing statements to alter or influence the application of the laws they sign. A line-item veto is a type of veto that keeps the majority of a spending bill unaltered but nullifies certain lines of spending within it. While a number of states allow their governors the line-item veto (discussed in the chapter on state and local government), the president acquired this power only in 1996 after Congress passed a law permitting it. President Clinton used the tool sparingly. However, those entities that stood to receive the federal funding he lined out brought suit. Two such groups were the City of New York and the Snake River Potato Growers in Idaho. The Supreme Court heard their claims together and just sixteen months later declared unconstitutional the act that permitted the line-item veto. Since then, presidents have asked Congress to draft a line-item veto law that would be constitutional, although none have made it to the president's desk.

On the other hand, signing statements are statements issued by a president when agreeing to legislation that indicate how the chief executive will interpret and enforce the legislation in question. Signing statements are less powerful than vetoes, though congressional opponents have complained that they derail legislative intent. Signing statements have been used by presidents since at least James Monroe, but they became far more common in this century.

National Security, Foreign Policy, and War

Presidents are more likely to justify the use of executive orders in cases of national security or as part of their war powers. In addition to mandating emancipation and the internment of Japanese Americans, presidents have issued orders to protect the homeland from internal threats. Most notably, Lincoln ordered the suspension of the privilege of the writ of habeas corpus in 1861 and 1862 before seeking congressional legislation to undertake such an act. Presidents hire and fire military commanders; they also use their power as commander-in-chief to aggressively deploy US military force. Congress rarely has taken the lead over the course of history, with the War of 1812 being the lone exception. Pearl Harbor was a salient case where Congress did make a clear and formal declaration when asked by FDR. However, since World War II, it has been the president and not Congress who has taken the lead in engaging the United States in military action outside the nation's boundaries, most notably in Korea, Vietnam, and the Persian Gulf.

Presidents also issue executive agreements with foreign powers. Executive agreements are formal agreements negotiated between two countries but not ratified by a legislature as a treaty must be. As such, they are not treaties under US law, which require two-thirds of the Senate for ratification. Treaties, presidents have found, are particularly difficult to get ratified. And with the fast pace and complex demands of modern foreign policy, concluding treaties with countries can be a tiresome and burdensome chore.

That said, some executive agreements do require some legislative approval, such as those that commit the United States to make payments and thus are restrained by the congressional power of the purse. But for the most part, executive agreements signed by the president require no congressional action and are considered enforceable as long as the provisions of the executive agreement do not conflict with current domestic law.

The Power of Persuasion

The framers of the Constitution, concerned about the excesses of British monarchial power, made sure to design the presidency within a network of checks and balances controlled by the other branches of the federal government. Such checks and balances encourage consultation, cooperation, and compromise in policymaking. This is most evident at home, where the Constitution makes it difficult for either Congress or the chief executive to prevail unilaterally, at least when it comes to constructing policy. Although much is made of political stalemate and obstructionism in national political deliberations today, the framers did not want to make it too easy to get things done without a great deal of support for such initiatives.

It is left to the president to employ a strategy of negotiation, persuasion, and compromise in order to secure policy achievements in cooperation with Congress. In 1960, political scientist Richard Neustadt put forward the thesis that presidential power is the power to persuade, a process that takes many forms and is expressed in various ways. Yet the successful employment of this technique can lead to significant and durable successes. For example, legislative achievements tend to be of greater duration because they are more difficult to overturn or replace, as the case of health care reform under President Barack Obama suggests. Obamacare has faced court cases and repeated (if largely symbolic) attempts to gut it in Congress. Overturning it will take a new president who opposes it, together with a Congress that can pass the dissolving legislation.

In some cases, cooperation is essential, as when the president nominates and the Senate confirms persons to fill vacancies on the Supreme Court, an increasingly contentious area of friction between branches. While Congress cannot populate the Court on its own, it can frustrate the president's efforts to do so. Presidents who seek to prevail through persuasion, according to Neustadt, target Congress, members of their own party, the public, the bureaucracy, and, when appropriate, the international community and foreign leaders. Of these audiences, perhaps the most obvious and challenging is Congress.

Much depends on the balance of power within Congress: Should the opposition party hold control of both houses, it will be difficult indeed for the president to realize his or her objectives, especially if the opposition is intent on frustrating all initiatives. However, even control of both houses by the president's own party is no guarantee of success or even of productive policymaking. For example, neither Bill Clinton nor Barack Obama achieved all they desired despite having favorable conditions for the first two years of their presidencies. In times of divided government (when one party controls the presidency and the other controls one or both chambers of Congress), it is up to the president to cut deals and make compromises that will attract support from at least some members of the opposition party without excessively alienating members of his or her own party. Both Ronald Reagan and Bill Clinton proved effective in dealing with divided government— indeed, Clinton scored more successes with Republicans in control of Congress than he did with Democrats in charge.

It is more difficult to persuade members of the president's own party or the public to support a president's policy without risking the dangers inherent in going public. There is precious little opportunity for private persuasion while also going public in such instances, at least directly. The way the president and his or her staff handle media coverage of the administration may afford some opportunities for indirect persuasion of these groups. It is not easy to persuade the federal bureaucracy to do the president's bidding unless the chief executive has made careful appointments. When it comes to diplomacy, the president must relay some messages privately while offering incentives, both positive and negative, in order to elicit desired responses, although at times, people heed only the threat of force and coercion.

While presidents may choose to go public in an attempt to put pressure on other groups to cooperate, most of the time they "stay private" as they attempt to make deals and reach agreements out of the public eye. The tools of negotiation have changed over time. Once chief executives played patronage politics, rewarding friends while attacking and punishing critics as they built coalitions of support. But the advent of civil service reform in the 1880s systematically deprived presidents of that option and reduced its scope and effectiveness. Although the president may call upon various agencies for assistance in lobbying for proposals, such as the Office of Legislative Liaison with Congress, it is often left to the chief executive to offer incentives and rewards. Some of these are symbolic, like private meetings in the White House or an appearance on the campaign trail. The president must also find common ground and make compromises acceptable to all parties, thus enabling everyone to claim they secured something they wanted.

Complicating Neustadt's model, however, is that many of the ways he claimed presidents could shape favorable outcomes require going public, which as we have seen can produce mixed results. Political scientist Fred Greenstein, on the other hand, touted the advantages of a "hidden hand presidency," in which the chief executive did most of the work behind the scenes, wielding both the carrot and the stick. Greenstein singled out President Dwight Eisenhower as particularly skillful in such endeavors.

Opportunity and Legacy

What often shapes a president's performance, reputation, and ultimately legacy depends on circumstances that are largely out of his or her control. Did the president prevail in a landslide or was it a closely contested election? Did he or she come to office as the result of death, assassination, or resignation? How much support does the president's party enjoy, and is that support reflected in the composition of both houses of Congress, just one, or neither? Will the president face a Congress ready to embrace proposals or poised to oppose them? Whatever a president's ambitions, it will be hard to realize them in the face of a hostile or divided Congress, and the options to exercise independent leadership are greater in times of crisis and war than when looking at domestic concerns alone.

Then there is what political scientist Stephen Skowronek calls "political time." Some presidents take office at times of great stability with few concerns. Unless there are radical or unexpected changes, a president's options are limited, especially if voters hoped for a simple continuation of what had come before. Other presidents take office at a time of crisis or when the electorate is looking for significant changes. Then there is both pressure and opportunity for responding to those challenges. Some presidents, notably Theodore Roosevelt, openly bemoaned the lack of any such crisis, which Roosevelt deemed essential for him to achieve greatness as a president.

People in the United States claim they want a strong president. What does that mean? At times, scholars point to presidential independence, even defiance, as evidence of strong leadership. Thus, vigorous use of the veto power in key situations can cause observers to judge a president as strong and independent, although far from effective in shaping constructive policies. Nor is such defiance and confrontation always evidence of presidential leadership skill or greatness, as the case of Andrew Johnson should remind us. When is effectiveness a sign of strength, and when are we confusing being headstrong with being strong? Sometimes, historians and political scientists see cooperation with Congress as evidence of weakness, as in the case of Ulysses S. Grant, who was far more effective in garnering support for administration initiatives than scholars have given him credit for.

These questions overlap with those concerning political time and circumstance. While domestic policymaking requires far more give-and-take and a fair share of cajoling and collaboration, national emergencies and war offer presidents far more opportunity to act vigorously and at times independently. This phenomenon often produces the rally around the flag effect, in which presidential popularity spikes during international crises. A president must always be aware that politics, according to Otto von Bismarck, is the art of the possible, even as it is his or her duty to increase what might be possible by persuading both members of Congress and the general public of what needs to be done.

Finally, presidents often leave a legacy that lasts far beyond their time in office. Sometimes, this is due to the long-term implications of policy decisions. Critical to the notion of legacy is the shaping of the Supreme Court as well as other federal judges. Long after John Adams left the White House in 1801, his appointment of John Marshall as chief justice shaped American jurisprudence for over three decades. No wonder confirmation hearings have grown more contentious in the cases of highly visible nominees. Other legacies are more difficult to define, although they suggest that, at times, presidents cast a long shadow over their successors. It was a tough act to follow George Washington, and in death, Abraham Lincoln's presidential stature grew to extreme heights. Theodore and Franklin D. Roosevelt offered models of vigorous executive leadership, while the image and style of John F. Kennedy and Ronald Reagan influenced and at times haunted or frustrated successors. Nor is this impact limited to chief executives deemed successful: Lyndon Johnson's Vietnam and Richard Nixon's Watergate offered cautionary tales of presidential power gone wrong, leaving behind legacies that include terms like *Vietnam syndrome* and the tendency to add the suffix "-gate" to scandals and controversies.

Summary

While the power of the presidency is typically checked by the other two branches of government, presidents have the unencumbered power to pardon those convicted of federal crimes and to issue executive orders, which don't require congressional approval but lack the permanence of laws passed by Congress. In matters concerning foreign policy, presidents have at their disposal the executive agreement, which is a much easier way for two countries to come to terms than a treaty that requires Senate ratification but is also much narrower in scope.

Presidents use various means to attempt to drive public opinion and effect political change. But history has shown that they are limited in their ability to drive public opinion. Favorable conditions can help a president move policies forward. These conditions include party control of Congress and the arrival of crises such as war or economic decline. But as some presidencies have shown, even the most favorable conditions don't guarantee success.

Presidents Can Accomplish a Great Deal with Executive Orders

Leighton Walter Kille

Leighton Walter Kille is cofounder of The Conversation France, *an online news organization whose mission is to give academics a greater voice in public affairs, as well as* Journalist's Resource, *a nonprofit project dedicated to bridging the gap between academia and journalism.*

Rick Kaplan kicked off his brown-bag talk, titled "The First 100 Days and the Press," by seemingly minimizing the importance of the very thing he'd come to talk about. "There's nothing magical about the first 100 days," he said. "It's a benchmark that journalists and writers have set up, because we always need to judge people."

Kaplan, executive producer for *CBS Evening News with Katie Couric*, noted that originally a president's first 100 days began not when he took the oath of office, but when Congress came into session. Why then? "Because there weren't as many executive orders being delivered as you see now, and the president's success was measured by how well he got along with Congress," he said.

Now a president can have the greatest impact immediately after taking oath and before his own team is set—Obama has less than 50 percent of his appointees in place, and while that means fewer hands on the levers of government, it also means less infighting.

"A lot of the things [presidents] want to do long term and a lot of things they feel in their hearts show up in the first 100 days," Kaplan said. For Bill Clinton that was gays in the military; for Obama it has been a list of things Kaplan called "extraordinary." He also singled out the president's performance at the recent G20 meeting.

"Kaplan: First 100 Days Has Shown What Obama Wants to Accomplish," by Leighton Walter Kille, Shorenstein Center, April 7, 2009. https://shorensteincenter.org/kaplan-first-100-days-has-shown-what-obama-wants-to-accomplish/. Licensed under CC by ND 3.0 Unported.

The immense size and global nature of the current crisis make the role of the press even more difficult than usual. "I actually had to learn what derivatives where," Kaplan joked. "This is really in-the-weeds, complicated stuff." Journalists don't always have the space or time to the go into the details, but they're exactly what the public needs to know. That's where the web can be a useful tool, allowing journalists to provide more information for those who want it, yet not slow things down for those who don't.

A significant portion of Kaplan's talk was spent addressing the current state of the media. A veteran of ABC News, MSNBC, and many other news organizations, Kaplan felt that the current economic climate had led to an increased responsibility in the media.

"These are serious times, and we can't afford to get into that era when there was so much noise coming out of the press corps toward the president, or the president toward the press corps. We can't afford that right now."

The President Can Declare War

Joel McDurmon

Joel McDurmon, PhD, is president of American Vision, a Christian nonprofit organization founded in 1978. He has authored more than twenty books.

As I wrote earlier this week, certain warmongers writing for *First Things* are concerned that not supporting Obama bombing Syria would set a "precedent of setting too low a threshold for blocking presidential initiative in foreign affairs," and this "is unwise." I interpreted this as a desire to keep the presidency strong in general, no matter what, so "that presidential prerogative to start wars without congressional approval will not be diminished."

This reason to support Obama in Syria, as I said, is an issue of Constitutional interpretation. As I wrote, "Most people in my circles believe that only Congress has the power to declare war." Rand Paul tried to exercise this argument against John Kerry during the Senate Committee hearings yesterday evening. He argued that it is "explicit" "throughout" Madison's writings that the power of war belongs to Congress and not the Executive. He stated, "This power is a congressional power and it is *not* an executive power."

While I support the spirit of peace and small government for which he is fighting, Paul is simply wrong. Whatever else Madison said, he *and all the constitutional framers* made exceptions to the general rule.

Yes, it's true, as Paul related, that Madison wrote, "The constitution supposes, what the History of all Govts demonstrates, that the Ex. is the branch of power most interested in war, & most prone to it. It has accordingly with studied care, vested the question of war in the Legisl."

But this was written in 1798 when the rival party was flirting with a war of which Madison disapproved. Of course he wanted to tie hands *then*. What Paul didn't relate was what Madison wrote

"Constitution: Yes, the President May Bomb Without Congressional Approval," by Dr. Joel McDurmon, American Vision, September 5, 2013. http://theono.my/1CQdHEO. Reprinted by permission.

next. He went on to decry the ability of the President to circumvent Congress *constitutionally* and start that war single-handedly anyway. Madison decried the effort, and the path he laid out would have been unwise on Adams' part, but it was nevertheless open to him. Referencing Madison here is therefore self-defeating to Paul's view.

Further, Madison's earlier writings strike a different tone. Not the least of these was his own tweaking of the constitutional article in question during the Convention. The original motion was to grant Congress the power "to make war" rather than "to declare war" as it eventually stood. Why? According to Madison's own notes, the discussion proceeded:

> Mr. Madison and Mr. Gerry moved to insert *"declare,"* striking out "make" war; *leaving to the Executive the power to repel sudden attacks.* . . .
>
> On the Motion to insert *declare*–in place of *Make,* it was agreed to.

The alleged "strict constructionist" Jefferson would later put those very powers to use. In his first Message to Congress in 1801, he explained his engagement of the Barbary pirates:

> I sent a small squadron of frigates into the Mediterranean, with assurances to that power of our sincere desire to remain in peace, but with orders to protect our commerce against the *threatened* attack. . . .
>
> One of the Tripolitan cruisers having fallen in with, and engaged the small schooner Enterprise, commanded by Lieutenant Sterret, which had gone as a tender to our larger vessels, was captured, after a heavy slaughter of her men, without the loss of a single one on our part.

Jefferson's narration goes on to show a delineation in his mind between what the president could do militarily with and without Congress:

> Unauthorized by the constitution, *without the sanction of Congress, to go out beyond the line of defence,* the vessel being disabled from committing further hostilities, was liberated with its crew. (Emphasis mine.)

But where in the document was this delineation expressly drawn? What are its boundaries? Unfortunately, *none are stated expressly*. It was assumed at the time to be between defense and aggression, but even this admits to various interpretations in various circumstances.

For this reason, upon hearing Jefferson's Message, Alexander Hamilton was distressed . . . by the restraint! He argued the President had the power to go ahead and also seize enemy property without sanction of Congress. He published a column called "The Examination," in which he castigated Jefferson for "a performance which ought to alarm all who are anxious for the safety of our Government, for the respectability and welfare of our nation." He reasoned:

> As it respects this conclusion [of the emergency of being attacked], the distinction between offensive and defensive war, makes no difference. . . .
>
> That instrument [the Constitution] has only provided affirmatively, that, "The Congress shall have power to declare War;" the plain meaning of which is that, it is the peculiar and exclusive province of Congress, *when the nation is at peace,* to change that state into a state of war. . . . But when a foreign nation declares, or openly and avowedly makes war upon the United States, they are then by the very fact, already *at war,* and any declaration on the part of Congress is nugatory: it is at least unnecessary.

Now, none of these men were addressing a situation similar to the one in Syria. The United States in no way has been attacked, and therefore there is no true "defense" on our part. Nor do we even have allies attacked, which is already beyond the specific issues addressed by Madison, Hamilton, etc. But just this far is enough to show the one basic principle: the power to make war—and you don't even have to call it a "police action" or "limited military action," you can just call it "war"—is not *exclusively* and *solely* vested in Congress. It is, in fact, *sometimes*, an Executive power, apart from Congress, and that is constitutional.

We have to deal with this, and the progression of it. Let's start with understanding it on the constitutional level.

What the Constitution Really Says

The "congress only" argument can only possibly be sustained through a strict constructionist view of the Constitution. But as I wrote yesterday,

> For whatever merits that view may have, it has been by far the minority view in practice in American history, was not practiced even by the framers who wrote the document, and indeed was thoroughly blown out of the waters of American jurisprudence by John Marshall in *McCulloch v. Maryland*, if not earlier. Hamilton was the most influential man in the first administration—the brains and energy behind Washington— and he never believed in strict construction for a moment.

No one paid any more than lip service to strict construction. First, the framers of the Constitution *purposefully* removed certain constraints from it, explicitly because they intended to allow any questionable issue to be defined and determined by the general government itself, not the states.

People deny this today. They do not want to accept that the Constitution was a vast centralization of powers. For example, one lawyer argued with me that the Tenth Amendment drew its language from the Articles of Confederation, and was intended therefore to constrain the federal government in behalf of the states to the same extent as the previous document, except where *expressly* enumerated. This is just simply wrong. The Tenth Amendment was a purposefully *denuded* version of the earlier arrangement, meant to buy off the States with similar but deceptive promises. Compare Article II of the Articles:

> Each state retains its sovereignty, freedom, and independence, and every power, jurisdiction, and right, which is not by this Confederation expressly delegated to the United States, in Congress assembled.

... with the Tenth Amendment:

> The powers not delegated to the United States by the Constitution, nor prohibited by it to the States, are reserved to the States respectively, or to the people.

Obviously the former statement is stronger in general, but do you notice the missing word in the Tenth that is *vital* in regard to construction? I have written about this before: it is the very word *expressly*. Contrast "expressly delegated" with "delegated," and ponder the potential differences in the hands of activist lawyers.

And what was John Marshall after all? When the question later arose whether a national bank could establish a branch within a state and defy the state's attempts to tax its profits, Marshall ruled that such an act would submit the federal bank beneath mere state jurisdiction—and the federal must remain supreme unless expressly denied in a certain area. And who gave this bank—not mentioned anywhere in the enumerated powers of the constitution, by the way—the right to such immunity? Marshall stuck it in their face in *McCulloch*:

> Even the 10th amendment, which was framed for the purpose of quieting the excessive jealousies which had been excited, omits the word 'expressly,' and declares only, that the powers 'not delegated to the United States, nor prohibited to the states, are reserved to the states or to the people;' thus leaving the question, whether the particular power which may become the subject of contest, has been delegated to the one government, or prohibited to the other, to depend on a fair construction of the whole instrument.

So even a strict construction of the Tenth Amendment at best leaves plenty of room for federal creativity, definition, etc., by virtue of its crafty wording. But in the truer reality of American history, as the establishment of the bank and Marshall's defense of it show, that creativity is almost limitless.

Second, now apply that principle and practice of interpretation to the war power of Congress in Article 1 Section 8: "The Congress shall have Power . . . To declare War. . . ." Paul, for example, was arguing adamantly about what this *doesn't* say. But this is self-defeating again. Granted, it *doesn't* say that the Executive has this power, but hey, it *doesn't* say that it doesn't have this power either. *All* it affirms is a certain power to Congress—it affirms nothing more and *denies* nothing *else.*

There is no negative power in regard to war for the executive anywhere in the Constitution. There is no express mention of it period, and this *at least* leaves it an open question in many ways. And that leads us to the last point here.

Third, with this principle and practice in mind, let's consider the President's job description in Article 2 Section 3: "he shall take Care that the Laws be faithfully executed."

Talk about a sea of undefined powers! What is "Care"? What does "take Care" mean ("Don't worry, Vito. I'll 'take care' of that guy for you.")? What "Laws" exactly? What is considered "faithful"? Who decides? Congress, the Supreme Court, popular vote, or the President himself?

And this is exactly noted by the early opponents of the constitution. William Symmes criticized early in the ratification debates in 1787:

> Can we exactly say how far a faithful execution of the laws may extend? or what may be called or comprehended in a faithful execution? If the President be guilty of a misdemeanor, will he not take care to have this excuse? And should it turn against him, may he not plead a mistake! or is he bound to understand the laws, or their operation? Should a Federal law happen to be as generally expressed as the President's authority; must he not interpret the Act! For in many cases he must execute the laws independent of any judicial decision. And should the legislature direct the mode of executing the laws, or any particular law, is he obliged to comply, if he does not think it will amount to a faithful execution? . . . Is there no instance in which he may reject the sense of the legislature, and establish his own, and so far, would he not be to all intents and purposes absolute?

So you see the president has considerable leeway in just *how* he interprets and executes the Laws. This is why we see Obama so often using apparently shady means to circumvent Congress when it's hostile to his agenda. Everyone shouts "Constitution! Constitution!" But it's the Constitution that gives him this very type of leeway.

Now, consider this power in light of the question of "what 'Laws'?" In this day and age the Executive is entrusted with the faithful execution of tens of thousands of pages of US Code and Administrative Law. This includes Treaties, nearly all foreign policy, and international law to which the US is a party. This means that very likely "defense" is no longer the *sole* criterion for Presidential prerogative in the use of force, or, at least, that the definition of the Word has expanded. It doesn't matter which, really.

Everyone knows this. The President since at least 1945 has had a wide range of circumstances in which he can deploy and use military force *without congressional approval*, and it's perfectly constitutional.

Breaking the Law

But let's suppose that whatever "Laws" might sanction Presidential lonewolfing in something like this Syria situation do not apply here. Let's say that whatever he wants to do, it sits right there outside of his powers, and he knows it. Do we have him trapped then?

Even then, Mr. Strict Constructionist himself, Jefferson, gives the president a pass in regard to existing law, whether strict construction, original intent, or not:

> A strict observance of the written laws is doubtless one of the high duties of a good citizen, but it is not the *highest*. The laws of necessity, of self-preservation, of saving our country when in danger, are of higher obligation. To lose our country by a scrupulous adherence to written law, would be to lose the law itself, with life, liberty, property and all those who are enjoying them with us; thus absurdly sacrificing the end to the means.

But what if the President wages a war and *Congress* uses its last resort: it refuses to fund that war. In a hypothetical consideration, Jefferson still gives prerogative to the president:

> Suppose it had been made known to the Executive of the Union in the autumn of 1805, that we might have the Floridas for a reasonable sum, that that sum had not indeed been so appropriated by law. . . . But suppose it foreseen that a John Randolph would find means to protract the proceeding on it by Congress, until the ensuing spring, by which time new circumstances would change the mind of the other party. Ought the Executive, in that case, and with that foreknowledge, to have secured the good to his country, and to have trusted to their justice for the transgression of the law? I think he ought, and that the act would have been approved.
>
> After the affair of the Chesapeake, we thought war a very possible result. Our magazines were illy provided with some necessary articles, nor had any appropriations been made for their purchase. We ventured, however, to provide them, and to place our country in safety; and stating the case to Congress, they sanctioned the act.

So much for "bind them down with the chains of the constitution!" Jefferson says the president sometimes should shoot first and ask forgiveness later.

But just so you don't think I alone am crazy, I was pleased to learn just this morning that the *libertarian* Judge Andrew Napolitano states the case, too. Speaking of Obama, he argues that the War Powers Resolution gives the President the power to act in Syria for a limited time *without congressional authorization:* "He knows that he already has the ability to engage in that without asking Congress." Even "if the Congress says no and the president does it anyway, *that will be consistent with federal law.*"

So, my strict constructionist friends, I hate to bear the news, but you are trapped not only by history, but also even by some of your heroes.

[…]

The President Shouldn't Be Able to Set Congress's Legislative Agenda

Max Bloom

Max Bloom is an editorial intern at National Review *and a student of mathematics and English literature at the University of Chicago.*

The accumulation of all powers legislative, executive, and judiciary, in the same hands, whether of one, a few, or many, and whether hereditary, self-appointed, or elective, may justly be pronounced the very definition of tyranny," James Madison wrote in *Federalist* No. 48. Montesquieu, quoted therein, warned that "when the legislative and executive powers are united in the same person or body, there can be no liberty, because apprehensions may arise lest the same monarch or senate should enact tyrannical laws to execute them in a tyrannical manner."

Madison and Montesquieu are perhaps not much remembered today. Separation of powers, once celebrated as a hallmark of the American experiment, is decidedly out of fashion. Our system delegates lawmaking to Congress, implementation to the executive, and the resolution of disputes to the courts, but there is a clamor to have it otherwise—everyone wants his preferred policies enacted and no one really trusts Congress with the job, so what does it matter if our constitutional order goes out the window in the service of a creative solution?

Barack Obama's presidency did not begin this phenomenon, but it serves as a useful example. Put aside even cases such as DACA, in which the president took it upon himself to pass large portions of the DREAM Act by executive order rather than through the cumbersome business of lawmaking. Put aside the Obamacare subsidies that Congress refused to appropriate and the administration "appropriated" in return.

"The President Shouldn't Set Congress's Legislative Agenda," by Max Bloom, *National Review*, June 23, 2017. Used with permission.

Put aside those particularly egregious cases, and just consider the signature policy achievements of Congress during Obama's tenure.

There is, first of all, Obamacare itself, proposed and substantially negotiated by Obama, drafted and conceived in large part by his aides. Then there is Dodd-Frank, which at least is not named after the president, but it so closely followed the administration's will that Obama said it "represents 90 percent of what I proposed when I took up this fight." Then there was the compromise that extended the Bush tax cuts in 2010, which followed almost precisely a framework agreement negotiated by Obama and Republican leadership. And there were the jobs bills Obama advertised in a speech to a joint session of Congress, declaring repeatedly that lawmakers should "pass this bill," even though no congressional committee had formulated any such "bill" at the time.

These were not isolated incidents, either. Remarkably, almost the entire legislative agenda of the Democratic Congress that governed between January 2009 and January 2011 was set by the president and implemented in close coordination with his administration—as if America were a parliamentary democracy and not a presidential republic. Such has been the expansion of the executive's power at the expense of the legislative's in the last few decades that this was seen as only natural. Think of how often Obamacare has been described as "Obama's signature legislation," or consider a few quotes from a more or less randomly chosen reflection on the president at Politico: on financial regulation, "Obama went on to push comprehensive Wall Street reforms through Congress"; on the stimulus, "he needed three GOP senators to avoid a filibuster, so he caved to their demands"; on jobs, "the same problem [of lacking the votes in Congress] stalled his American Jobs Act."

Obamacare and the American Jobs Act, of course, can't be "Obama's" legislation, because the president doesn't legislate; likewise, it should be strange to talk of Obama's modifying a bill to accede to Republican demands, or of his pushing a bill through

Congress. But none of these sentences sounds at all strange to us: That's just what presidents do nowadays. They push bills through Congress; they negotiate with political opponents to craft a successful law; they even take public "ownership" of the legislation "they" pass. That is the vocabulary of the present era.

Perhaps this explains why there has been so much confusion about Trump's relationship with Congress. Trump, unlike Obama, is neither conversant in legislative policy nor particularly interested in it nor even all that interested in marketing his own agenda to Congress. And so signature pieces of legislation, such as the AHCA or, presumably, the forthcoming tax-reform proposal, have been conceived of and managed by the House and the Senate, with only intermittent coordination with the executive branch.

In response, critics have seemed confused. Take Glenn Thrush, who tweeted that "for all the bombast, Trump presidency defined by historic ceding of power to Congress. Ryan set the agenda. Mitch is filling in the details." This, of course, is incoherent. You can't cede power you don't have, and Trump does not, as a matter of the Constitution, have the power to set the legislative agenda. Then there are those who simply cannot process the fact that legislation nowadays comes from Congress. Into this camp we may place anyone who insists on referring to the AHCA as "Trumpcare" despite Trump's manifest lack of interest in its details or, most likely, in the repeal of Obamacare at all. "Ryancare" is far more apt, but less popular, since policymaking is now thought of as a presidential preserve.

If the point of politics is to get your preferred policy implemented, consequences be damned, and your party controls the White House, it is useful to have the president's allies in Congress act primarily as a voting bloc for his proposals. The president commands an immense amount of authority and prestige—far more, generally, than congressional leaders—and so will have an easier time unifying the party and mobilizing the electorate. Moreover, he is concerned about his legacy and insulated from many of the petty congressional preoccupations that have always bothered Americans—the frequent pace of elections, the need to forge long-term relationships, the pet projects, the local constituents—so his proposals tend to be more ambitious and more inspiring. This is why liberals were so unperturbed by Obama's involvement in the legislative process, and it is why many conservatives have been frustrated by Trump's failure to help guide Republican lawmaking.

But think of Madison and Montesquieu. Though their concerns may seem idealistic now, in our age of partisan warfare, it's worth remembering that the Constitution already disposes to the president a tremendous amount of power. The power to enforce the laws carries with it a great enough potential for abuse; it is downright dangerous to gift the president the power to write the laws as well.

It is true that most of the safeguards in the Constitution are still operative. The president must still secure the requisite votes in Congress for his legislation to pass, for instance, and Congress still retains the power to impeach him. But the separation of powers, properly construed, is more than simply procedural: Its basis, as Madison famously argued, is in the way that each branch of government is drawn by pride and ambition to limit the other branches of government.

This has worked well for much of American history—think of the aforementioned War Powers Resolution or of Henry Cabot Lodge's struggle with Wilson over the League of Nations or of the formation of the Whig Party in opposition to the executive aggrandizements of Andrew Jackson. But it is inconsistent with a state of affairs where partisans in Congress see themselves as subordinate to a friendly White House. Whenever the president effectively writes a piece of legislation and Congress dutifully passes it, the natural competition between the two branches erodes slightly and they began to view each other more as allies than as distinct political units working in tension with each other. It is a worrisome commentary on the condition of American politics that many pundits have begun to ignore this tension completely and view, say, House Republicans as the policymaking wing of the Trump administration.

This is not to say, of course, that there is no room for coordination between the OMB and the Senate over tax reform, or that Trump's lack of interest in mastering the details of health-care reform is healthy. The president will naturally be involved in policymaking to some degree, the executive branch can offer useful guidance to lawmakers, and parties must coordinate their actions internally. But it is no tragedy that the path to health-care reform so far has been navigated by Paul Ryan and Mitch McConnell rather than by Trump.

It's just the proper way of things.

Current
CONTROVERSIES

2

Do Executive Orders Work against the Three-Branch Political System?

The Expressed and Expanded Powers of the President

Lumen Learning

Lumen Learning's mission is to make learning opportunities available to all students, regardless of socioeconomic background, by using open educational resources (OER) to create well-designed and low-cost course materials that replace expensive textbooks.

Expressed Powers

The expressed powers of the President are those expressed in the Constitution of the United States.

President and Vice President

Article Two of the United States Constitution creates the executive branch of the government, consisting of the president, the vice president, and other executive officers chosen by the president. Clause 1 states that "the executive Power shall be vested in a President of the United States of America. He shall hold his Office during the Term of four Years, and, together with the Vice President, chosen for the same Term, be elected, as follows." Clause one is a "vesting clause," similar to other clauses in Articles 1 and 3, but it vests the power to execute the instructions of Congress, which has the exclusive power to make laws.

Clause 2 states the method for choosing electors in the Electoral College. Under the US Constitution the president and vice president are chosen by electors, under a constitutional grant of authority delegated to the legislatures of the states and the District of Columbia. In other words, the constitution lets the state legislatures decide how electors are created. It does not define or delimit what process a state legislature may use to create its state's college of electors. In practice, since the 1820s, state

"The Powers of the Presidency," Lumen Learning. https://courses.lumenlearning.com/boundless-politicalscience/chapter/the-powers-of-the-presidency/. Licensed under CC by 4.0 International.

legislatures have generally chosen to create electors through an indirect popular vote. Each state chooses as many electors as it has Representatives and Senators in Congress. Under the Twenty-third Amendment, the District of Columbia may choose no more electors than the state with the lowest number of electoral votes. Senators, Representatives, or federal officers may not become electors.

Presidential Powers

Perhaps the most important of all presidential powers is commander-in-chief of the United States Armed Forces. While the power to declare war is constitutionally vested in Congress, the president commands and directs the military and is responsible for planning military strategy. Congress, pursuant to the War Powers Resolution, must authorize any troop deployments longer than 60 days, although that process relies on triggering mechanisms that never have been employed, rendering it ineffectual. Additionally, Congress provides a check on presidential military power through its control over military spending and regulation. While historically presidents initiated the process for going to war, critics have charged that there have been several conflicts in which presidents did not get official declarations, including Theodore Roosevelt's military move into Panama in 1903, the Korean War, the Vietnam War, and the invasions of Grenada in 1983 and Panama in 1990. The "wars" waged in Iran (2001) and Afghanistan since (2003) are officially called "military engagements" authorized by Congress. Officially, the US was not at war with the governments of those nations, but fought non-government terrorist groups.

Along with the armed forces, the president also directs US foreign policy. Through the Department of State and the Department of Defense, the president is responsible for the protection of Americans abroad and of foreign nationals in the United States. The president decides whether to recognize new nations and new governments, and negotiates treaties with other nations, which become binding on the United States when approved by a two-thirds vote of the Senate.

The president is the head of the executive branch of the federal government and is constitutionally obligated to "take care that the laws be faithfully executed. " Generally, a president may remove purely executive officials at his discretion. However, Congress can curtail and constrain a president's authority to fire commissioners of independent regulatory agencies and certain inferior executive officers by statute. To manage the growing federal bureaucracy, presidents have gradually surrounded themselves with many layers of staff who were eventually organized into the Executive Office of the President of the United States.

The president also has the power to nominate federal judges, including members of the United States courts of appeals and the Supreme Court of the United States. However, these nominations require Senate confirmation. Securing Senate approval can provide a major obstacle for presidents who wish to orient the federal judiciary toward a particular ideological stance. When nominating judges to US district courts, presidents often respect the long-standing tradition of Senatorial courtesy.

The Constitution's Ineligibility Clause prevents the president from simultaneously being a member of Congress. Therefore, the president cannot directly introduce legislative proposals for consideration in Congress. However, the president can take an indirect role in shaping legislation, especially if the president's political party has a majority in one or both houses of Congress. For example, the president or other officials of the executive branch may draft legislation and then ask senators or representatives to introduce these drafts into Congress. The president can further influence the legislative branch through constitutionally mandated, periodic reports to Congress. These reports may be either written or oral, but today are given as the State of the Union address, which often outlines the president's legislative proposals for the coming year.

Delegated Powers

The delegated powers are a list of items found in the US Constitution that set forth the authoritative capacity of Congress.

Introduction

Almost all presidential powers rely on what Congress does or does not do. Presidential executive orders implement the law, but Congress can overrule such orders by changing the law. And many presidential powers are delegated powers that Congress has accorded presidents to exercise on its behalf and that it can cut back or rescind.

Delegated Powers

The delegated powers, also called enumerated powers, are a list of items found in Article I, Section 8 of the US Constitution that set forth the authoritative capacity of Congress. In summary, Congress may exercise the powers that the Constitution grants it, subject to explicit restrictions in the Bill of Rights and other protections in the Constitution. The Tenth Amendment states that "The powers not delegated to the United States by the Constitution, nor prohibited by it to the States, are reserved to the States respectively, or to the people. " Historically, Congress and the Supreme Court of the United States have broadly interpreted these provisions.

The list of enumerated powers includes the following: "The Congress shall have Power To lay and collect Taxes, Duties, Imposts and Excises, to pay the Debts and provide for the common Defence and general Welfare of the United States; but all Duties, Imposts and Excises shall be uniform throughout the United States;" "To borrow Money on the credit of the United States;" "to declare War, grant Letters of Marque and Reprisal, and make Rules concerning Captures on Land and Water;" and "to make all Laws which shall be necessary and proper for carrying into Execution the foregoing Powers, and all other Powers vested by this Constitution in the Government of the United States, or in any Department or Officer thereof."

Political Interpretation

There is a difference of opinion in the political arena on whether current interpretation of enumerated powers, as exercised by Congress, is constitutionally sound. One school of thought is called "strict constructionism." Strict constructionists often reference a statement on the enumerated powers set forth by Chief Justice Marshall in the case *McCulloch v. Maryland*. Strict constructionism refers to a particular legal philosophy of judicial interpretation that limits or restricts judicial interpretation. The phrase is also commonly used more loosely as a generic term for conservatism among the judiciary.

Another school of thought is referred to as "loose constructionism." Loose constructionists provide a wider and broader reading of the Constitution and amendments passed historically.

Interpretation of the Necessary and Proper Clause has been controversial, especially during the early years of the republic. Strict constructionists interpret the clause to mean that Congress may make a law only if the inability to do so would cripple its ability to apply one of its enumerated powers. Loose constructionists, on the other hand, interpret the Necessary and Proper Clause as expanding the authority of Congress to all areas tangentially related to one of its enumerated powers.

Inherent Powers

Inherent powers are assumed powers of the president not specifically listed in the Constitution.

Inherent powers are those powers that a sovereign state holds. In the United States, the President derives these powers from the loosely worded statements in the Constitution that "the executive Power shall be vested in a President" and that the President should "take care that the laws be faithfully executed"; defined through practice rather than through constitutional or statutory law. In other words, Inherent powers are assumed powers of the president not specifically listed in the Constitution. Inherent powers come from the president's role as chief executive.

The first three presidents, Washington, Adams, and Jefferson established their importance in different ways. First, Washington helped to establish them in the first place, when he wanted to use them as a basis for proclaiming a policy of strict neutrality when the British and French were at war. Then, due to Adams poor leadership skills, the Federalists and Anti-Federalists divisions were heightened and the development of political parties was quickened. Finally, Jefferson used the party system to cement strong ties with Congress and expanded the role of the president in the legislative process. He used the inherent powers to justify the Louisiana Purchase in 1803 which dramatically increased the size of our nation.

The question of presidential power is complicated by a key omission in certain Constitutional sentences' language. As opposed to Article 1, which states that Congress is vested with the legislative powers "herein granted," Article 2 does not use that language. It says all executive power is vested in the president. Supporters of the unitary executive theory argue that this means that the president's power, particularly the inherent power that come with being commander in chief, are open ended and cannot be checked by the other two branches.

Emergency Powers

The president of the United States, as head of the executive branch, has the authority to declare a federal state of emergency.

Introduction

A state of emergency is a governmental declaration that may suspend some normal functions of the executive, legislative, and judicial powers; alert citizens to change their normal behaviors; or order government agencies to implement emergency preparedness plans. It also can be used as a rationale for suspending rights and freedoms, even if guaranteed under the Constitution. Such declarations usually come during a time of natural or man-made disaster, periods of civil unrest, or following a declaration of war or situation of international or internal armed conflict.

Application in the United States

In the United States, there are several methods for government response to emergency situations. A state governor or local mayor may declare a state of emergency within his or her jurisdiction. This is common at the state level in response to natural disasters. The president of the United States, as head of the executive branch, has the authority to declare a federal state of emergency. At least two constitutional rights are subject to revocation during a state of emergency: The right of habeas corpus, under Article 1, Section 9, and the right to a grand jury for members of the National Guard when in actual service, under Fifth Amendment.

Habeas corpus was suspended on April 27, 1861 during the American Civil War by Abraham Lincoln in parts of Maryland and some midwestern states, including southern Indiana. He did so in response to demands by generals to set up military courts to rein in "copperheads," those in the Union who supported the Confederate cause. On December 16, 1950, during the Korean War, President Truman issued Presidential Proclamation No. 2914, declaring a state of national emergency. In 1952, the Supreme Court ruling in *Youngstown Sheet & Tube Co. v. Sawyer* established that presidents may not act contrary to Acts of Congress during an emergency.

The Insurrection Act of 1807 is the set of laws that govern the president's ability to deploy troops within the United States to put down lawlessness, insurrection, and rebellion. The general aim is to limit presidential power as much as possible, relying on state and local governments for initial response in the event of insurrection. Coupled with the Posse Comitatus Act, presidential powers for law enforcement are limited and delayed.

During the Watergate scandal, which erupted in the 1970s after President Richard Nixon authorized a variety of illegal acts, Congress investigated the extent of the president's powers and belatedly realized that the United States had been in a continuous state of emergency since 1950. As a result, in 1976, the

National Emergencies Act set a limit of two years on emergency declarations unless the president explicitly extends them and requires the president to specify in advance which legal provisions will be invoked. The act terminated the emergency of 1950 on September 14, 1978; however, even in the twenty-first century, the federal courts have upheld harsh penalties for crimes that occurred during the state of national emergency from 1950 to 1978, where the penalties were escalated because of the existence of that emergency.

Executive Orders

In the United States, an executive order is an order or directive issued by the head of the executive branch at some level of government.

Introduction

In the United States, an executive order is an order or directive issued by the head of the executive branch at some level of government. The term executive order is most commonly applied to orders issued by the President, who is the head of the executive branch of the federal government. Executive orders may also be issued at the state level by a state's governor or at the local level by the city's mayor.

US Presidents have issued executive orders since 1789, usually to help officers and agencies of the executive branch manage the operations within the federal government itself. Executive orders have the full force of law, since issuances are typically made in pursuance of certain Acts of Congress. Typically, these specifically delegate to the President a degree of discretionary power, or are believed to take authority from a power granted directly to the Executive by the Constitution. However, these perceived justifications cited by Presidents when authoring Executive Orders have come under criticism for exceeding Executive authority; at various times throughout US history, challenges to the legal validity or justification for an order have resulted in legal proceedings.

Basis in US Constitution

Although there is no Constitutional provision or statute that explicitly permits executive orders, there is a vague grant of executive power given in Article II, Section 1, Clause 1 of the Constitution, and furthered by the declaration "take Care that the Laws be faithfully executed" made in Article II, Section 3, Clause 5. Most executive orders use these Constitutional interpretations as the authorization allowing for their issuance to be justified as part of the President's sworn duties. The intention is to help direct officers of the US Executive carry out their delegated duties as well as the normal operations of the federal government: the consequence of failing to comply possibly being the removal from office.

Different Applications by President

A Presidential Determination is a document issued by the White House stating a determination resulting in an official policy or position of the executive branch of the United States government. Presidential determinations may involve any number of actions, including setting or changing foreign policy, setting drug enforcement policy, or any number of other exercises of executive power. One of the most famous presidential determinations was President Clinton's Presidential Determination 95-45, which exempted the US Air Force's facility in the vicinity of Groom Lake, Nevada (commonly called Area 51) from environmental disclosure laws, in response to subpoenas from a lawsuit brought by Area 51 workers alleging illegal hazardous waste disposal which resulted in injury and death. Subsequent to this determination, the lawsuit was dismissed due to lack of evidence.

Similarly, presidential memoranda do not have an established process for issuance or publication. Presidential memoranda are generally considered less prestigious than executive orders. There are three types of memorandum: presidential determination or presidential finding, memorandum of disapproval, and hortatory memorandum.

Finally, a presidential proclamation "states a condition, declares a law and requires obedience, recognizes an event or triggers the implementation of a law (by recognizing that the circumstances in law have been realized)." Presidents define situations or conditions on situations that become legal or an economic truth. These orders carry the same force of law as executive orders—the difference between the two is that executive orders are aimed at those inside government while proclamations are aimed at those outside government. The administrative weight of these proclamations is upheld because they are often specifically authorized by congressional statute, making them "delegated unilateral powers." Presidential proclamations are often dismissed as a practical presidential tool for policymaking because of the perception of proclamations as largely ceremonial or symbolic in nature. However, the legal weight of presidential proclamations suggests their importance to presidential governance.

Executive Privilege

Executive privilege is the power claimed by the President to resist subpoenas and other interventions by other branches of government.

Introduction

In the United States government, executive privilege is the power claimed by the President of the United States and other members of the executive branch to resist certain subpoenas and other interventions by the legislative and judicial branches of government. The concept of executive privilege is not mentioned explicitly in the United States Constitution, but the Supreme Court of the United States ruled it to be an element of the separation of powers doctrine, and/or derived from the supremacy of the executive branch in its own area of Constitutional activity.

The Supreme Court confirmed the legitimacy of this doctrine in *United States v. Nixon*, but only to the extent of confirming that there is a qualified privilege. Once invoked, a presumption of privilege is established, requiring the prosecutor to make a "sufficient showing" that the "Presidential material" is "essential to the justice of the case. " Historically, the uses of executive privilege underscore the untested nature of the doctrine, since Presidents have generally sidestepped open confrontations with the United States Congress and the courts over the issue by first asserting the privilege, then producing some of the documents requested on an assertedly voluntary basis.

Historical Development

During the period of 1947–49, several major security cases became known to Congress. There followed a series of investigations, culminating in the famous Hiss-Chambers case of 1948. At that point, the Truman Administration issued a sweeping secrecy order blocking congressional efforts from the FBI and other executive data on security problems. During the Army–McCarthy hearings in 1954, Eisenhower used the claim of executive privilege to forbid the "provision of any data about internal conversations, meetings, or written communication among staffers, with no exception to topics or people. " Department of Defense employees were also instructed not to testify on any such conversations or produce any such documents or reproductions.

US v. Nixon

The Supreme Court addressed "executive privilege" in *United States v. Nixon*, the 1974 case involving the demand by Watergate special prosecutor Archibald Cox that President Richard Nixon produce the audiotapes of conversations he and his colleagues had in the Oval Office of the White House in connection with criminal charges being brought against members of the Nixon Administration. Nixon invoked the privilege and refused to produce any records. Because Nixon had asserted only a generalized need for confidentiality, the Court held that the larger public interest in obtaining the truth in the context of a criminal prosecution took precedence.

Post-Nixon

The Clinton administration invoked executive privilege on fourteen occasions. In 1998, President Bill Clinton became the first President since Nixon to assert executive privilege and lose in court, when a federal judge ruled that Clinton aides could be called to testify in the Lewinsky scandal.

Correspondingly, the Bush administration invoked executive privilege on six occasions. President George W. Bush first asserted executive privilege to deny disclosure of sought details regarding former Attorney General Janet Reno, the scandal involving the Federal Bureau of Investigation (FBI) misuse of organized-crime informants James J. Bulger and Stephen Flemmi in Boston, and Justice Department deliberations about President Bill Clinton's fundraising tactics, in December 2001. On August 1, 2007, Bush invoked the privilege for the fourth time in little over a month, this time rejecting a subpoena for Karl Rove. The subpoena would have required the President's Senior Advisor to testify before the Senate Judiciary Committee in a probe over fired federal prosecutors.

On June 20, 2012, President Barack Obama asserted executive privilege, his first, to withhold certain Department of Justice documents related to the ongoing Operation Fast and Furious controversy ahead of a United States House Committee on Oversight and Government Reform vote to hold Attorney General Eric Holder in Contempt of Congress for refusing to produce the documents. Later the same day, the United States House Committee on Oversight and Government Reform voted 23–17 along party lines to hold Attorney General Holder in contempt of Congress over not releasing documents regarding Fast and Furious.

The Expansion of Presidential Powers

Presidential power has shifted over time, which has resulted in claims that the modern presidency has become too powerful.

Chief Legislator

The President of the United States of America is the head of state and head of government of the United States. The president leads the executive branch of the federal government and is the commander-in-chief of the United States Armed Forces.

Powers and Duties

The first power the Constitution confers upon the president is the veto. The Presentment Clause requires any bill passed by Congress to be presented to the president before it can become law. Perhaps the most important of all presidential powers is command of the United States Armed Forces as commander-in-chief. While the power to declare war is constitutionally vested in Congress, the president commands and directs the military and is responsible for planning military strategy. Congress, pursuant to the War Powers Resolution, must authorize any troop deployments longer than 60 days, although that process relies on triggering mechanisms that have never been employed, rendering it ineffectual. Additionally, Congress provides a check to presidential military power through its control over military spending and regulation.

The president is the head of the executive branch of the federal government and is constitutionally obligated to "take care that the laws be faithfully executed." The executive branch has over four million employees, including members of the military. Presidents make numerous executive branch appointments—an incoming president may make up to 6,000 before he takes office and 8,000 more during his term. Ambassadors, members of the Cabinet, and other federal officers are all appointed by a president with the "advice and consent" of a majority of the Senate. Appointments made while the Senate is in recess are temporary and expire at the end of the next session of the Senate.

Historically, two doctrines concerning executive power have developed that enable the president to exercise executive power with a degree of autonomy. The first is executive privilege, which allows the president to withhold from disclosure any communications made directly to the president in the performance of executive duties. George Washington first claimed executive privilege when Congress requested to see Chief Justice John Jay's notes from an unpopular treaty negotiation with Great Britain. While not enshrined in the Constitution, or any other law, Washington's action created the precedent for the privilege. When Richard Nixon tried to use executive privilege as a reason for not turning over subpoenaed evidence to Congress during the Watergate scandal, the Supreme Court ruled in *United States v. Nixon*, 418 U.S. 683 (1974) that executive privilege did not apply in cases where a president was attempting to avoid criminal prosecution. When President Bill Clinton attempted to use executive privilege regarding the Lewinsky scandal, the Supreme Court ruled in *Clinton v. Jones*, 520 U.S. 681 (1997) that the privilege also could not be used in civil suits. These cases established the legal precedent that executive privilege is valid, although the exact extent of the privilege has yet to be clearly defined. Additionally, federal courts have allowed this privilege to radiate outward and protect other executive branch employees, but have weakened this protection for those executive branch communications that do not involve the president.

Critics of Enhanced Presidency

Most of the nation's Founding Fathers expected the Congress, which was the first branch of government described in the Constitution, to be the dominant branch of government. In other words, they did not expect a strong executive. However, presidential power has shifted over time, which has resulted in claims that the modern presidency has become too powerful, unchecked, unbalanced, and "monarchist" in nature. Critic Dana D. Nelson believes presidents over the past thirty years have worked towards "undivided presidential control of the executive branch and its agencies." She criticizes proponents of the unitary executive for expanding "the many existing uncheckable executive powers—such as executive orders, decrees, memorandums, proclamations, national security directives and legislative signing statements—that already allow presidents to enact a good deal of foreign and domestic policy without aid, interference or consent from Congress." Other scholars disagree with the view that the presidency has too much power and cite the ability of Congress and the courts to block presidential actions. As an example, the Supreme Court in 2016 overturned Pres. Obama's administrative appointment made during a Congressional recess, and is scheduled to rule on the constitutionality of an executive order know as DACA (Deferred Action for Childhood Arrivals) that delays deportation of undocumented residents who arrived as children.

The Separation of Powers Must Be Maintained

Jason Pye

Jason Pye is the vice president of legislative affairs for FreedomWorks, a conservative and libertarian advocacy group based in Washington, DC.

While the 115th Congress begins on January 3 at noon, President Barack Obama will continue to serve in the White House until January 20, when President-elect Donald Trump takes office. The first 100 days of the incoming administration are expected to be incredibly busy. Obviously, the repeal of ObamaCare is at the top of the congressional to-do list, and action to begin this effort is expected to be immediate. Reining in the regulatory state is another item on which action is projected to be swift.

Congress passed several pieces of legislation over the last two years that aggressively take on the regulatory state and begin the process of restoring Article I of the Constitution, and it is likely that these bills will be reintroduced and come up for votes in the early days of the 115th Congress:

H.R. 712 - Sunshine for Regulatory Decrees and Settlements Act: The Sunshine for Regulatory Decrees and Settlements Act reforms the practice known as "sue and settle," in which outside groups supportive of regulations sue the federal government and settle out of court behind closed doors, resulting in an agreement that brings new regulations. The bill passed the House in January 2015 by a vote of 244 to 173. It was never brought up for a vote in the Senate.

H.R. 427 - Regulations from the Executive in Need of Scrutiny (REINS) Act: The REINS Act subjects major rules and regulations—those with an annual cost of $100 million or more—to congressional approval. The bill passed the House in July 2015 by a vote of 243 to 165. It was never brought up for a vote in the Senate.

"Restoring the Separation of Powers Through Congressional Action, Reversing Executive Orders and Regulations," by Jason Pye, Freedom Works, December 19, 2016. Reprinted by permission.

H.R. 4768 - Separation of Powers Restoration Act: The Separation of Powers Restoration Act reverses the *Chevron* doctrine created by the Supreme Court in 1984. The *Chevron* doctrine allows federal courts to defer to federal regulatory agencies' interpretations of perceived ambiguities in federal law. The bill would reverse this egregious doctrine established by the Supreme Court and force federal courts to rule on regulations based on merit, not deference. The Separation of Powers Restoration Act passed the House in July 2016 by a vote of 240 to 171. The bill was never brought up for a vote in the Senate.

H.R. 5982 - Midnight Rules Relief Act: The Midnight Rules Relief Act allows Congress to consider bring up a resolution that would disapprove of multiple regulations finalized by federal regulatory agencies within the 60 legislative days allowed by Congressional Review Act. The bill passed the House in November 2016 by a vote of 240 to 179. It was never brought up for a vote in the Senate.

In addition to action by Congress under the Congressional Review Act and other legislative initiatives that can reverse regulation, the incoming administration can begin to undo Obama-era rules by executive action and new regulations, according to the Competitive Enterprise Institute's Wayne Crews. It is worth noting that undoing a regulation is not an easy task. The same process used to promulgate a regulation, including comment periods, is required to roll it back.

Still, there is no shortage of regulations the Trump administration can target. The House Freedom Caucus, for example, recently rolled out a list of more than 200 regulations that its members would like to see reversed. "These last 8 years, we have seen a disturbing trend of the federal government unnecessarily inserting themselves more and more into the lives of hardworking Americans—and the results have been economically disastrous," House Freedom Caucus Chairman Mark Meadows (R-N.C.) said in a release that included the list of regulations. "When the American people spoke on November 8, they provided conservatives with an opportunity to restore order in our government and to remove the out-of-control bureaucratic red tape that so often stunts the growth of otherwise successful Americans.

"My colleagues and I look forward to helping President-elect Trump in any way we can as we work toward the most productive 'first 100 days' in modern history. To the working people who have felt the burden of these last 8 years so heavily—help is on the way," he added.

The list contains tens of billions of dollars' worth of rules, regulations, and executive orders that Chairman Meadows and the House Freedom Caucus want to see undone, from the Food and Drug Administration's nutrition standards for school lunches to the administration's directive undermining work requirements for food stamps to the Federal Communications Commission's net neutrality rule to Internal Revenue Service's death tax regulations to carbon emissions rules promulgated by the Environmental Protection Agency.

Most of the rules, regulations, and executive orders—at least those that have dates listed in the report—were enacted or promulgated during the Obama administration, and most of them are past the 60 legislative days that the Congressional Review Act allows Congress to disapprove of a rule or regulation. It will take legislative action to statutorily reverse an executive or regulatory action or it must go through the regulatory process from start to finish, which will take a significant amount of time.

Certainly, the effort to restore Article I and the constitutional separation will not be rapid. After all, the growth of executive power and the regulatory state has occurred over decades and is not limited to any single administration. Indeed, each administration comes into power viewing the floor left by its predecessor as a floor, not a ceiling, which is something of which Congress needs to be mindful, regardless of which party is in control of the White House. But the legislative ideas are there to reverse the trend, as is a list of regulations, thanks to Chairman Meadows and the House Freedom Caucus, to reverse the trend of executive and regulatory power.

The Use and Abuse of Executive Orders Throughout History

Todd Gaziano

Todd Gaziano is Executive Director of Pacific Legal Foundation's Washington, DC Center and Senior Fellow in Constitutional Law. He has served in all three branches of the federal government and is a well-known scholar and leader in the liberty legal movement.

I n recent years, there has been renewed interest in the proper use and possible abuse of executive orders and other presidential directives. Many citizens and lawmakers expressed concern over the content and scope of several of President Bill Clinton's executive orders and land proclamations. Congress responded with hearings and the consideration of several bills designed to curb the President's authority to issue such directives. In an exceedingly rare act, the courts reacted by striking down one of President Clinton's executive orders, and litigation to contest the validity of other directives is ongoing.

Despite the increased public attention focused on executive orders and similar directives, public understanding regarding the Legal foundation and proper uses of such presidential decrees is limited. Thus, the increased public attention generally has been accompanied by confusion and occasional misunderstandings regarding the legality and appropriateness of various presidential actions. This Legal memorandum provides a general overview of the President's use of executive directives, including a discussion of the historical practice, the sources of presidential authority, the Legal framework of analysis, and reform proposals related to the use and abuse of presidential directives.

"The Use and Abuse of Executive Orders and Other Presidential Directives," by Todd Gaziano, Heritage Foundation, February 21, 2001. Reprinted by permission.

The Separation of Powers

[…]

Moreover, defenders of executive authority will find much in President Clinton's use of executive orders and proclamations that is instructive—even if they dispute the lawfulness or policy goals of the individual decrees. In short, some helpful lessons can be learned from recent experience about how an aggressive President can use his power for appropriate and beneficial purposes, and these lessons can help guide the current and future Presidents of the United States in making executive decisions.

In the end, the constitutional separation of powers supports both sides of the argument over a President's proper authority. It reinforces a President's right or duty to issue a decree, order, or proclamation to carry out a particular power that truly is committed to his discretion by the Constitution or by a lawful statute passed by Congress. On the other hand, the constitutional separation of powers cuts the other way if the President attempts to issue an order regarding a matter that is expressly committed to another branch of government; it might even render the presidential action void. Finally, separation of powers principles may be unclear or ambiguous when the power is shared by two branches of government.

Thus, no simple recitation of governing law or prudential guidelines is possible. However, History and practice are useful tools in understanding the President's authority, and a Legal framework of analysis exists to help determine issues of validity. Beyond questions of legality, there are many separate but important issues of policy. Two broad policy questions present themselves: (1) whether a given power the President possesses ought to be used to advance a particular policy objective, and (2) whether a particular draft directive effectively advances such a policy goal.

Defining Presidential Directives

In order to place these issues of legality and policy in their proper context, it is important to start with an understanding of the nature and historical usage of such executive decrees.

From the founding of this nation, American Presidents have developed and used various types of presidential or executive "directives." The best known directives are executive orders and presidential proclamations, but many other documents have a similar function and effect. Reduced to their common core, presidential directives simply are written, rather than oral, instructions or declarations issued by the President. Because we would not expect or want the President to limit himself solely to oral instructions and declarations, it is not surprising that every President has used written directives to run the executive branch of government.

Early Presidential Directives

On June 8, 1789, three months after he was sworn in as President of the United States, George Washington sent an instruction to the holdover officers of the Confederation government asking each of them to prepare a report "to impress me with a full, precise, and distinct general idea of the affairs of the United States" that they each handled. Although the term "executive order" was not used until 1862, President Washington's instruction was the precursor of the executive order and was unquestionably proper. Every chief executive has the inherent power to order subordinates to prepare reports for him on the performance of their duties. The United States Constitution expressly provides that the President may require his principal officers to prepare such reports.

A few months later, a joint committee of Congress requested that President Washington "recommend to the people of the United States a day of public thanksgiving." On October 3, 1789, President Washington responded with a proclamation urging the people to recognize Thursday, November 26, 1789, as the day of thanksgiving. Heads of state had issued proclamations commemorating victorious battles and national holidays for centuries, and there was no reason for Congress or the President to conclude that the Constitution removed this ceremonial function from our head of state. Congress may go farther than the President and pass laws fixing a particular holiday and granting paid leave to federal employees, but the President is free in the absence of congressional action to recommend such celebrations as he sees fit.

Executive orders also have been used to direct foreign policy since the presidency of George Washington, when he issued a proclamation in 1793 stating that the United States would be "friendly and impartial toward the belligerent powers" of Britain and France. In this "Neutrality Proclamation," Washington justified his power to issue such a statement based on the "law of nations," but a firmer ground would have been the constitutional powers vested in the President over foreign affairs. Washington, with the concurrence of Secretary of State Thomas Jefferson and Secretary of the Treasury Alexander Hamilton, did not convene the Congress to debate the proclamation before issuing it. James Madison, among others, criticized Washington's proclamation as an overextension of executive authority and an infringement on Congress's authority to decide issues of war and peace. Congress later gave approval to Washington's course of action by passing the Neutrality Act of 1794, at Washington's request, giving the President the power to prosecute violators of the proclamation. However, this early episode demonstrates that the President and Congress may have overlapping responsibilities, and in such situations, the scope of the President's power to act unilaterally is sometimes unclear.

Sources of Presidential Authority

Although President Washington's Thanksgiving Proclamation was hortatory, other proclamations or orders communicate presidential decisions that have a legally binding effect. Authority for these directives must come from either the Constitution or statutory delegations.

On August 7, 1794, President Washington issued a proclamation ordering those engaged in the Whiskey Rebellion to disperse and calling forth the militia to put down the rebellion. This proclamation was issued pursuant to statutory authority delegated to the President. The statute provided that the President first had to warn citizens to disperse and return to their homes, but that he could call forth the militia to deal with any individuals who did not follow this command. Thus, the Whiskey Rebellion Proclamation may have been the first directive issued pursuant to power conferred by Congress.

On December 25, 1868, President Andrew Johnson issued a proclamation (the "Christmas Proclamation") pardoning "all and every person who directly or indirectly participated in the late insurrection or rebellion" related to the Civil War. President Johnson's Christmas Proclamation was grounded squarely on his constitutional pardon power. The Supreme Court subsequently ruled that the proclamation was "a public act of which all courts of the United States are bound to take notice, and to which all courts are bound to give effect."

As the Christmas Proclamation demonstrates, the President's authority to issue written directives is not limited to express language in the Constitution that grants him power to issue such directives. The President possesses additional authority to issue directives where that is the reasonable implication of the power granted (implied authority) or if it is inherent in the nature of the power conferred (inherent authority). The term "Commander in Chief of the Army and Navy" (as used in Article II of the Constitution) necessarily implies that the commander can issue oral and written commands, and it is inherent in the nature of a military commander that he do so.

If the President's authority is implied or inherent in a statutory grant of power, Congress remains free to negate or modify the underlying authority. Congress also has some latitude in defining or refining the procedures the President must take in the exercise of that authority, although there are some constitutional limits to Congress's power to micromanage executive branch decision-making procedures.

When the President is exercising powers inherent in Article II of the Constitution, Congress has much less ability to regulate or circumscribe the President's use of written directives. Some of President Clinton's claims of implied and inherent authority were outrageous. The US Court of Appeals for the District of Columbia Circuit struck down one of his executive orders that was based on such an overly broad claim, demonstrating that a President's claim that he is exercising inherent constitutional power will not always prevail. But when the President really is exercising a legitimate constitutional power—for example, his authority as Commander in Chief—Congress and the courts have little or no say in how the President communicates his commands.

Legitimate Uses of Presidential Directives

As the foregoing discussion suggests, there are many legitimate uses of presidential directives. The following functions of the President expressly mentioned in the US Constitution are among the more important under which the President may issue at least some directives in the exercise of his constitutional and statutorily delegated powers:

- Commander in Chief. The President's power as Commander in Chief is limited by other constitutional powers granted to Congress, such as the power to declare war, raise and support the armed forces, make rules (i.e., laws) for the regulation of the armed forces, and provide for calling forth the militia of the several states. However, the President's power as military commander is still very broad with respect to the armed forces at his disposal, including some situations in which Congress has not acted to declare war.
- Head of State. The President is solely responsible for carrying out foreign policy, which includes the sole power to recognize

foreign governments, receive foreign ambassadors, and negotiate treaties. Congress may enact laws affecting foreign policy, and two-thirds of the Senate must ratify any treaty before it becomes binding law, but Congress must still leave the execution of foreign policy and diplomatic relations to the President.

- Chief Law Enforcement Officer. The President has the sole constitutional obligation to "take care that the laws be faithfully executed," and this grants him broad discretion over federal law enforcement decisions. He has not only the power, but also the responsibility to see that the Constitution and laws are interpreted correctly. In addition, the President has absolute prosecutorial discretion in declining to bring criminal indictments. As in the exercise of any other constitutional power, one may argue that a particular President is "abusing his discretion," but even in such a case, he cannot be compelled to prosecute any criminal charges.

- Head of the Executive Branch. The Framers debated and rejected the creation of a plural executive. They selected a "unitary executive" and determined that he alone would be vested with "[t]he executive power" of Article II. After much debate, the Framers also determined that the President would nominate and appoint (with the Senate's consent in some cases) all officers in the executive branch. With very few exceptions, all appointed officials who work in the executive branch serve at the will and pleasure of the President, even if Congress has specified a term of years for a particular office. All of this was designed to ensure the President's control over officials in the executive branch and to promote "energy in the executive."

When the President is *lawfully* exercising one of these functions, the scope of his power to issue written directives is exceedingly broad. In short, he may issue or execute whatever written directives, orders, guidelines (such as prosecutorial guidelines or nondiscriminatory enforcement policies), communiqués, dispatches, or other instructions he deems appropriate.

The President also may issue directives in the exercise of his statutorily delegated authority, unless Congress has specified in law that the statutory power may be exercised only in a particular way. A few examples of Congress's conditional grant of statutory authority are mentioned herein, but as previously explained, there are limits to how far Congress can go in an attempt to micromanage even the President's statutorily delegated authority. For example, Congress can grant the President (or his Attorney General) the authority to deport certain illegal aliens, but it cannot attempt to retain a veto over the final decision as it tried to do in the Immigration and Nationality Act.

In sum, a President has broad discretion to use written directives when he is lawfully exercising one of his constitutional or statutorily delegated powers. Any broad power or discretion can be abused, but it would be wrong to confuse such potential or real abuse with the many legitimate uses.

[...]

The US Government Has a Constitutional Duty to Supervise

Gillian E. Metzger

Gillian E. Metzger is the Stanley H. Fuld Professor of Law at Columbia Law School. She writes and teaches in the areas of constitutional law, administrative law, and federal courts.

The Internal Revenue Service (IRS) targets applications for nonprofit tax-exempt status by organizations using the name "Tea Party" for special scrutiny.[1] The National Security Agency (NSA) repeatedly violates governing privacy requirements and oversteps its authority in conducting surveillance.[2] Recently opened online federal health exchanges fail to function, preventing individuals from signing up for health insurance or determining their eligibility for benefits.[3] Officials at some Veterans Administration (VA) hospitals manipulate data to hide long delays in scheduling appointments, and there are allegations that some veterans died while on waiting lists.[4]

A key theme that links these examples is that they all involve managerial and supervisory failure. Most commonly, the problem is too little supervision,[5] but sometimes the concern is too much supervision or supervision of the wrong kind.[6] The Obama Administration's experience is hardly unique; similar lists of instances of failed oversight exist for prior administrations and at all levels of government.

The central importance of supervision should not come as a surprise. Supervision and other systemic features of government administration with which it overlaps—planning, policy-setting, monitoring, resource allocation, institutional structures, personnel systems, and the like—are fundamental in shaping how an agency operates and its success in meeting its statutorily

"The Constitutional Duty to Supervise," by Gillian E. Metzger, *Yale Law Journal*, April 2015. Reprinted by permission.

imposed responsibilities.[7] These systemic features are also precisely what distinguish administrative government. Agencies not only adjudicate individual cases, take specific enforcement actions, or issue discrete rules. They do all these activities on a massive scale as part of a broader project of law implementation that requires coordination, investigation, and prioritization.[8] Moreover, if anything, the importance of administration is only more acute today than it has been historically, with new approaches to program implementation and regulation resulting in a broader array of actors wielding greater discretionary authority, often in contexts lacking external controls like judicial review.[9] As a result, systemic features of administration—in particular, internal supervision through planning and ongoing monitoring—are increasingly the linchpin for achieving accountability of federal government programs and actions.[10]

Multiple avenues exist for addressing management and supervisory failures. The recent IRS, NSA, VA, and Health and Human Services (HHS) debacles have triggered extensive media coverage, internal and independent investigations, resignations, proposed legislation, and lawsuits, and they may ultimately lead to criminal prosecutions.[11] One route of response that comes much less quickly to mind than these options, however, is constitutional law. Indeed, the centrality of systemic administration in practice contrasts starkly with its virtual exclusion from contemporary US constitutional doctrine. The exclusion of administration takes a variety of doctrinal guises, such as restrictive standing requirements, individualistic mens rea requirements, and limitations on respondeat superior and supervisory liability in suits against government officers.[12] To be sure, there are exceptions: procedural due process challenges and institutional reform litigation represent two instances in which administrative and systemic functioning play a more central role in assessing whether constitutional requirements are violated. But in many ways these exceptions prove the rule, as judicial resistance to engaging with administration has led courts to view the exceptions quite narrowly.[13]

In short, constitutional law stands largely aloft from the reality of administrative governance, with the Supreme Court refusing to subject systemic features of government operations to constitutional scrutiny. I use constitutional law here to refer to judicially determined constitutional doctrine. This is not to deny that constitutional doctrine represents only one dimension of constitutional law. It is judicially enforced constitutional law, as opposed to forms of constitutional law that emerge from the actions of Congress and the President, or constitutional understandings generated by other actors such as administrative agencies, state and local governments, and social movements.[14] Yet despite the scholarly attention paid to non-judicial constitutional law of late, the courts continue to play a dominant role as expositors of constitutional meaning. And their willingness to defer to constitutional interpretation by other branches appears, if anything, to be dwindling.[15] As a result, the courts' resistance to incorporating administration serves to exclude it from our most recognized form of constitutional interpretation and perpetuates the view that general aspects of administration fall outside the Constitution's ambit.

In this Article, I argue that the exclusion of systemic administration from constitutional law is a mistake.[16] This exclusion creates a deeply troubling disconnect between the realities of government and constitutional requirements imposed on exercises of governmental power. Authorizing and controlling governmental action, along with establishing the federal government's structure, are critical constitutional functions.[17] Incorporating systemic administration is essential if the Constitution is to perform these functions in ways that are responsive to modern governance.

Furthermore, the current doctrinal exclusion of administration stands at odds with the Constitution. The Constitution specifies few details of federal administrative government, but its text and structure repeatedly emphasize one particular systemic administrative feature: supervision. This emphasis on supervision manifests itself most prominently in Article II's imposition on the President of a duty to "take Care that the Laws be faithfully executed,"[18] but also surfaces more broadly as a constitutional prerequisite for delegation of governmental power, rooted in separation of powers principles and due process. With such delegation comes responsibility to supervise so as to ensure that the transferred authority is used in a constitutional and accountable fashion. A central claim of this Article is that the Constitution embodies a duty to supervise that current doctrine has simply failed to acknowledge. The precise contours of this duty vary depending on how one conceives of its constitutional basis. A version of the duty based on Article II demands supervision by and within the executive branch, while a version based on principles of delegation extends supervisory obligations to the courts, Congress, and potentially the states. But under both accounts, a duty to supervise represents a basic precept of our federal constitutional structure.

Systemic features of administration thus carry huge practical import and substantial constitutional salience. What then explains their exclusion from constitutional law? The answer is separation of powers concerns and fears of overstepping the judicial role. The Supreme Court put the point bluntly in *Lewis v. Casey*, insisting that "it is not the role of courts, but that of the political branches, to shape the institutions of government in such fashion as to comply with the laws and the Constitution."[19] The Court has elsewhere emphasized that "[t]he Constitution . . . assigns to the Executive Branch, and not to the Judicial Branch, the duty to 'take Care that the Laws be faithfully executed.'"[20] Moreover, the concern is not just with respecting the purview of the political branches but also with protecting the courts, because overseeing administration and managing government institutions are not tasks for which the courts have much institutional competence. Courts both lack political accountability and have little expertise in running administrative institutions or in navigating the substantive policy areas at stake.

These concerns about judicial role and competency are real, but they do not justify the Supreme Court's current refusal to engage with systemic administration. In particular, the challenges that courts would face in directly enforcing a constitutional duty to supervise do not support refusing to recognize that such a duty exists. Direct judicial enforcement sometimes may be appropriate, even if difficult, and recognizing that a supervisory duty exists may open up important avenues for indirect enforcement through subconstitutional law. In addition, recognition of a constitutional duty to supervise may actually serve to mitigate some concerns about judicial aggrandizement. Perhaps most importantly, given the current dominance of the courts in determining constitutional meaning, judicial recognition of a constitutional duty to supervise is critical even if responsibility for enforcing this duty falls entirely on the political branches.

Indeed, recognizing a constitutional duty to supervise is as central to the overall project of constitutional interpretation as it is to better connecting constitutional law to the realities of contemporary governance. The judicial-role concerns implicated by the duty to supervise underscore the need for greater attention to ways in which courts can support constitutional enforcement by the political branches. Recognizing such a duty also highlights the porous boundary between constitutional and subconstitutional law, with statutory or administrative law disputes increasingly functioning as mechanisms for constitutional articulation. Acknowledging this constitutional-subconstitutional interplay and theorizing its proper bounds should be a central focus of contemporary constitutional law and scholarship.

This Article aims to demonstrate the constitutional significance of systemic administration and justify recognition of a constitutional duty to supervise. Such recognition should come from all the branches, and it is notable that President Obama recently referenced his "constitutional duty to supervise the executive branch" in a signing statement.[21] But recognition of the duty is particularly needed from the courts, given their preeminent role in constitutional interpretation and their current flawed rejection of administration's constitutional relevance. Critically, however, judicial recognition does not automatically translate into direct judicial enforcement. Judicial recognition fosters enforcement by Congress and the President by putting the political branches on notice of their constitutional obligations. Moreover, to the extent judicial enforcement occurs, it will commonly be indirect—by means of administrative law. Indeed, recognizing the constitutional duty to supervise will likely have its greatest import as a basis for reframing current administrative-law doctrines and analysis, which—like current constitutional law—insistently exclude administration from their reach.

[...]

Notes

1. See Jonathan Weisman, *Management Flaws at I.R.S. Cited in Tea Party Scrutiny*, N.Y. TIMES, May 14, 2013, http://www.nytimes.com/2013/05/15/us/politics/report-on-irs-audits -cites-ineffective-management.html [http://perma.cc/C4FN-FL6M].

2. Barton Gellman, *NSA Broke Privacy Rules Thousands of Times Per Year, Audit Finds*, WASH. POST, Aug. 15, 2013, http://www.washingtonpost.com/world/national-security/nsa-broke -privacy-rules-thousands-of-times-per-year-audit-finds/2013/

3. *See* Robert Pear et al., *From the Start, Signs of Trouble at Health Portal*, N.Y. TIMES, Oct. 12, 2013, http://www.nytimes.com/2013/10/13/us/politics/from-the-start-signs-of-trouble-at -health-portal.html [http://perma.cc/JL7M-G6D6].

4. *See* Richard A. Oppel Jr. & Michael D. Shear, *Severe Report Finds V.A. Hid Waiting Lists at Hospitals*, N.Y. TIMES, May 28, 2014, http://www.nytimes.com/2014/05/29/us/va-report -confirms-improper-waiting-lists-at-phoenix-center.html [http://perma.cc/73JM-BR9F].

5. *See* Carol D. Leonnig, *Court: Ability To Police U.S. Spying Program Limited*, WASH. POST, Aug. 15, 2013, http://www.washingtonpost.com/politics/court-ability-to-police-us-spying -program-limited/2013/08/15/4a8c8c44-05cd-11e3-a07f-49ddc7417125_story.html [http:// perma.cc/9XWB-4JJK] (discussing limits on the oversight capacity of the Foreign Intelligence Surveillance Court); Oppel & Shear, *supra* note 4 (noting that an investigation revealed VA hospital administrators were responsible for manipulating waiting lists); Pear et al., *supra*

note 3 (noting the limited capacity of the agency overseeing development of the federal health exchange); Weisman, *supra* note 1 (reporting that a Treasury inspector general blamed the IRS's inappropriate tea party targeting on ineffective IRS management).

6. *See* Pear et al., *supra* note 3 (identifying the impact of White House political considerations and last-minute decisions on the flawed rollout of the exchanges); *see also* Robert J. Delahunty & John C. Yoo, *Dream On: The Obama Administration's Nonenforcement of Immigration Laws, the DREAM Act, and the Take Care Clause,* 91 TEX. L. REV. 781, 784-85 (2013) (faulting President Obama for initiating a policy that granted immunity to a large group of young illegal aliens).

7. *See* PATRICIA W. INGRAHAM ET AL., GOVERNMENT PERFORMANCE: WHY MANAGEMENT MATTERS 2, 8 (2003); Jerry L. Mashaw, *Foreword: The American Model of Federal Administrative Law: Remembering the First One Hundred Years,* 78 GEO. WASH. L. REV. 975, 992 (2010) (noting that "in many ways, it is the internal law of administration—the memos, guidelines, circulars, and customs within agencies—that mold most powerfully the behavior of federal officials").

8. Edward Rubin, *It's Time To Make the Administrative Procedure Act Administrative,* 89 CORNELL L. REV. 95, 97, 100-37 (2003).

9. *See infra* Part I.B.

10. *See* Rubin, *supra* note 8, at 97; William Simon, *The Organizational Premises of Administrative Law* 6, 12 (Columbia Law Sch. Pub. Law & Legal Theory Working Paper Grp., Paper No. 13-356, 2013), http://ssrn.com/abstract=2332079 [http://perma.cc/872T-PYUK].

11. *See, e.g.,* Richard A. Oppel, Jr., *Official Says Prosecutors Are Looking at V.A. Lists,* N.Y. TIMES, May 15, 2014, http://www.nytimes.com/2014/05/16/us/politics/veterans-secretary-shinseki -to-testify-on-long-waits-for-patients.html [http://perma.cc/S3J7-3QUQ].

12. *See infra* Part I.C.

13. *See infra* notes 92-97, 121-127, 133-135 and accompanying text.

14. *See generally* JACK BALKIN, LIVING ORIGINALISM (2011); WILLIAM N. ESKRIDGE, JR. & JOHN FEREJOHN, A REPUBLIC OF STATUTES: THE NEW AMERICAN CONSTITUTION (2010); KEITH E. WHITTINGTON, CONSTITUTIONAL CONSTRUCTION: DIVIDED POWERS AND CONSTITUTIONAL MEANING (1999); Gillian E. Metzger, *Administrative Constitutionalism,* 91 TEX. L. REV. 1897 (2013); Robert Post & Reva Siegel, *Roe Rage: Democratic Constitutionalism and Backlash,* 42 HARV. C.R.-C.L. L. REV. 373 (2007).

15. *See, e.g.,* United States v. Windsor, 133 S. Ct. 2675, 2686 (2013) (expressing concern that "the Supreme Court's primary role in determining the constitutionality of a law that has inflicted real injury on a plaintiff . . . would become only secondary to the President's" if the President's agreement that a challenged statute was unconstitutional were enough to preclude judicial

review); Shelby Cnty. v. Holder, 133 S. Ct. 2612, 2631 (2013) (rejecting Congress's determination that the Voting Rights Act's trigger for requiring preclearance was an appropriate means of enforcing the constitutional prohibition on racial discrimination in voting); Zivotofsky *ex rel.* Zivotofsky v. Clinton, 132 S. Ct. 1421, 1427-30 (2012) (rejecting the claim that the constitutionality of a statute regulating foreign relations represented a political question outside of the courts' purview). *But see* NLRB v. Noel Canning, 134 S. Ct. 2550, 2559-60 (2014) (emphasizing the weight given to historical political-branch practice in separation of powers disputes).

16. The same point is true of administration's exclusion from administrative law doctrines, as several scholars have recently argued. *See* Daniel A. Farber & Anne Joseph O'Connell, *The Lost World of Administrative Law*, 92 TEX. L. REV. 1137, 1140 (2014); Sidney A. Shapiro, *Why Administrative Law Misunderstands How Government Works: The Missing Institutional Analysis*, 53 WASHBURN L.J. 1 (2013); Simon, *supra* note 10. In addition, some scholars have criticized the divide between administration and administrative-law doctrine from a public administration standpoint and offered accounts that assign public administration and public management a constitutional role. *See* ANTHONY M. BERTELLI & LAURENCE E. LYNN, JR., MADISON'S MANAGERS: PUBLIC ADMINISTRATION AND THE CONSTITUTION 12, 103-66 (2006); JOHN A. ROHR, TO RUN A CONSTITUTION: THE LEGITIMACY OF THE ADMINISTRATIVE STATE 15-53 (1986).

17. *See* Richard H. Fallon, Jr., *Constitutional Constraints*, 97 CALIF. L. REV. 975, 987-95 (2009).

18. U.S. CONST. art. II, § 3.

19. 518 U.S. 343, 349 (1996); *see also* Bell v. Wolfish, 441 U.S. 520, 548, 562 (1979) ("[T]he operation of our correctional facilities is peculiarly the province of the Legislative and Executive Branches of our Government, not the Judicial.").

20. Allen v. Wright, 468 U.S. 737, 761 (1984).

21. *See* Barack Obama, *Statement by the President on H.R. 4310,* WHITE HOUSE (Jan. 3, 2013), http://www.whitehouse.gov/the-press-office/2013/01/03/statement-president-hr-4310 [http://perma.cc/KU3J-YYJG].

Without Executive Orders, Political Polarization Would Prevent Anything from Being Accomplished

William P. Marshall

William P. Marshall is currently the Kenan Professor of Law at the University of North Carolina. He was Deputy White House Counsel and Deputy Assistant to the President of the United States during the Clinton administration.

I t may be hard to look over the current political landscape without concluding that some remedy for the current political dysfunction is in order. We live in a time when political polarization is so intense that some members of one party have openly stated that they would do virtually anything to block the agenda of the sitting President—up to and including opposing members of their own caucus who suggest that some compromises with the other side might be in order. These politicians have lived up to their words. The President's agenda in Congress has been stalled, and many of the serious problems facing the nation remain unanswered.

The President has not stayed on the sidelines while his opponents have done all they can to make his presidency fail. Rather, he has engaged in a series of unilateral actions across a range of spectrums in an attempt to circumvent the political roadblocks placed before him—a strategy that he coined "We Can't Wait." These actions have included, among others, an aggressive use of the recess appointment power, selective enforcement of certain statutory provisions such as those in the Affordable Care Act and the Immigration and Nationality Act, and the use of signing statements, rather than the veto, to signal that the President would not comply with what he believed to be constitutionally objectionable limitations imposed on his authority by the Congress.

"Warning!: Self-Help and the Presidency," by William P. Marshall, *Yale Law Journal*, October 29, 2014. Reprinted by permission.

Not surprisingly, many of the President's opponents (and at times some of his defenders) have claimed that such uses of unilateral executive branch power violate constitutional boundaries. The Obama Administration, in turn, has staunchly defended its actions as constitutionally permissible, and in so doing has relied on the traditional lines of legal authority pertaining to the scope of presidential power. This has not been an easy task. The Court's recent decision in *NLRB v. Noel Canning*, invalidating the President's expansive use of his recess appointment authority, is but one example in which an attempt to defend the President's actions on traditional legal grounds has not proved successful.

David Pozen would make the job of an Obama Administration lawyer a whole lot easier. In *Self-Help and the Separation of Powers* (*"Self-Help"*), Pozen argues that, when Congress acts wrongly, the President may permissibly take actions that are outside her normal constitutional bounds. This means, according to Pozen, that the President, in addition to possessing her other powers, may enjoy the remedy of self-help as a legitimate response to congressional obstreperousness. An Administration lawyer could therefore, under Pozen's theory, defend a President's otherwise "extra-legal" actions as a permissible response to an asserted "failure of congressional lawmaking" without having to point to any direct constitutional allocation of authority to the executive branch.

When I first read an early draft of *Self-Help*, I told the author that I believed it to be one of the most brilliant and innovative pieces of law review scholarship that I had ever encountered. I also told him that I thought it was possibly one of the most dangerous. The last thing American constitutional law needs is another rationale that could be used to justify an expansive exercise of executive branch power, particularly when that exercise is based on little more than a President's own conclusion that Congress has somehow engaged in constitutional wrongdoing when it aggressively seeks to frustrate her agenda.

The final version of *Self-Help* confirmed my earlier convictions. The Article is wonderfully accomplished and is a testament to

Pozen's skills as a legal scholar. At the same time, however, the thesis advanced in *Self-Help* remains alarming. The modern presidency has already (and long since) ascended to the role of the most dangerous branch. Allocating to the presidency the additional tool of self-help along with its already formidable arsenal would only exacerbate the considerable imbalance among the branches that already exists.

[...]

One point before proceeding: Pozen, of course, recognizes that introducing the self-help justification into the law of separation of powers will create the danger of an undue expansion in presidential power. But he also contends that notions of self-help are already at play in interbranch relations and that bringing the law of self-help explicitly to the fore would not so much change existing interbranch behavior as it would provide legal structure for an existing dynamic. As such, presumably, the acknowledgment of the role of self-help in separation of powers would not necessarily create new risks of presidential aggrandizement; it would only make more explicit the hazards that already exist.

If this is indeed Pozen's argument, however, then it both overstates the role that an inchoate regime of self-help currently plays in separation of powers and understates the effects that would accrue if the availability of the self-help remedy were formally recognized. Certainly, Pozen may be correct as a descriptive matter that, at times, a frustrated President or Congress may believe that the purported malfeasance of the other justifies an extraordinary response. But he is incorrect to the extent that he suggests this belief has become an accepted legal justification for an extraordinary exertion of power. Consider the illustrations raised by Pozen as examples where the use of self-help by the President might have been justified: President Obama's uses of his recess appointment power and selective enforcement authority in response to Congressional intransigence. In none of those instances did President Obama assert that his actions were legal as a result of congressional obstruction. Instead, he claimed his actions were within the formal bounds of his authority. Even more to the point, neither the Office of Legal Counsel (OLC) nor the Solicitor General (SG), as Pozen acknowledges, have ever even argued that a President's actions can be defended on the basis of self-help or any similar doctrine (although both offices are not exactly known for being shy about asserting executive branch prerogative). The *Self-Help* thesis then is not the recognized law of the land and, if accepted, would move the law of interbranch relations onto new ground.

That new ground, moreover, is likely to prove particularly fertile for presidential power expansion. As the law now stands, a President is at least inhibited from taking otherwise impermissible action because of the precariousness of acting outside the formal constitutional bounds of her authority without legal justification. The recognition of a right of self-help, however, would provide the President with a direct license to proceed. And, as discussed in Part II below, this is a license that the President will be tempted to use early and often.

I. Congressional Obstruction as a Constitutional Wrong

Whether the President should have the power of self-help to overcome unconstitutional congressional obstructionism obviously depends in part on whether congressional obstructionism is actually a constitutional wrong. Pozen's *Self-Help* suggests that it is, or at least that it can be, because it arguably violates interbranch constitutional conventions. The assertion that congressional obstruction actually transgresses constitutional norms, however, is questionable.

To begin with, congressional obstruction has been around for as long as there has been a Congress. From the first congressional session in 1789, members have used dilatory tactics to fight presidential actions that they opposed. To be sure, the current efforts of some in the Republican congressional caucus to thwart President Obama arguably have taken opposition tactics to an extreme—at least with respect to the breadth of the blockade of the President's agenda. Many Republicans seem quite seriously committed not only to opposing the President's policies, but also to doing all they can, in the words of one prominent conservative commentator, to make sure that his presidency fails.

Nevertheless, even this sort of "maximalist obstructionism" is not so easily characterized as outside the bounds of permissible congressional behavior. Rather, congressional prerogative to block executive action is an essential component of the constitutional design. Although Pozen suggests, with some support, that the Framers believed that separation of powers would promote governmental efficiency, their more central concern was with facilitating the ability of one branch to impede the other rather than with promoting interbranch cooperation. As Justice Brandeis famously noted, the Framers sought an arrangement "not to promote efficiency but to preclude the exercise of arbitrary power." And as the Court recently reaffirmed in Noel Canning, "[The Constitution] is not designed to overcome serious institutional friction . . . . [F]riction between the branches is an inevitable consequence of our constitutional structure."

Second, the conclusion that obstruction is a constitutional wrong is not supported by history. As referenced previously, congressional efforts to obstruct Presidents have been common occurrences throughout our nation's history. Filibusters or similar tactics have been used by Senate minorities to oppose majority actions since the beginning of the Republic. Presidents Herbert Hoover, Franklin Roosevelt, and Harry Truman faced notably obstructionist Congresses during the middle of the last century. More recently, congressional Democrats did all they could to block the efforts of President George W. Bush to privatize Social Security, although that proposal was a central part of his agenda. Similarly Democratic Senator Paul Wellstone, before he died prematurely in a plane crash, endeavored to use every congressional procedure possible to prevent the United States from going to war in Iraq. The constitutional convention regarding congressional obstruction, if there is one, may actually be that doing all that one can to prevent the enactment of measures that one opposes is a central part of American politics.

Third, it is not even clear that the extreme position of acting (or refusing to act) to deliberately cause a presidency to fail is constitutionally inappropriate. To begin with, such extreme action is not completely unprecedented. The congressional opponents of President Martin Van Buren, for example, were dedicated to ensuring that his presidency was short-lived. Congressional intransigence did not begin with the election of President Obama.

Fourth, the obduracy of the congressional Republicans may simply be a sign of the times. We now live in an era of the so-called permanent campaign; each side sees itself in constant electoral war with the other. To the opposition party, a successful administration can often lead to the victory of the President's party in the next election cycle and, in fact, presidential actions are commonly taken with the next election in mind. Accordingly, from a purely political perspective, if not from a good government stance, the strategy of doggedly blocking the President at every turn is completely understandable. Arguably, then, Congress may not be acting wrongly even under an understanding that posits unwritten norms can set rules of interbranch behavior. The current political norm has become simply one of incessant partisan warfare.

Finally, the contention that Congress acts outside its bounds when it thwarts the executive seems particularly weak in the context of legislation. The Constitution, after all, places the primary role in promulgating legislation with the Congress; the role of the President, by contrast, is merely to recommend legislation. The contention that Congress obstructs (or can obstruct) a President when it blocks her legislative agenda is therefore arguably misplaced because Congress is the key movant in the legislative process.

II. Self-Help and the Power of the Presidency

The major problem with the self-help thesis, however, is less the claim that congressional obstruction should be considered a constitutional wrong than the suggestion that the President's acting extra-legally should be deemed a constitutional right. Even if congressional obstruction can be fairly characterized as a violation of constitutional conventions in some circumstances, the dangers of granting the tool of self-help to the President to respond to those infractions outweigh any possible benefits. Part II.A demonstrates why—even though Pozen's thesis allows any aggrieved branch to use the weapon of self-help—the primary beneficiary of the remedy is likely to be the President. Part II.B shows why placing that weapon in the hands of the executive is so perilous.

Why the Self-Help Remedy Will Primarily Empower the President

Under Pozen's thesis, the self-help remedy is nominally available to both Congress and the executive, but the likelihood is that it will primarily benefit the latter. To begin with, as Pozen notes, the President will be consistently favored in her ability to take extra-legal measures because she will be unencumbered by collective action concerns. Unlike the Congress, the President can act unilaterally, and, unlike the Congress, the executive branch is not divided along partisan lines. Additionally, unlike the Congress, the President can act quickly and seize the moment when taking a particular action is most politically expedient. By timing her actions effectively, she can minimize any political blowback that might otherwise accrue in a way that Congress—with its cumbersome procedures—cannot. Further, compared to Congress, the President is likely to be under-deterred in taking such measures because, outside of political objections, the responses of the other branches to her actions will be limited. Many of the President's actions are unlikely to be reviewable by the courts because individual litigants will have difficulty demonstrating the particularized harm necessary for Article III standing, and after *Raines v. Byrd*, it is unlikely that the Senate, the House of Representatives, or individual members of Congress will have standing either. Congress, meanwhile, will be hampered in its responses to a President's use of self-help because of collective action problems.

Congress, moreover, will be far less able to use self-help to take actions that violate large-C (or formal) constitutional constraints for the simple reason that it is unclear what effective extra-legal large-C measures Congress could undertake. After all, obstructing a President's agenda by not moving legislation or by refusing to confirm nominees is not a violation of large-C constitutional requirements even if, as Pozen asserts, such actions can or do violate constitutional conventions. There are no formal constitutional constraints on Congress's refusal to pass laws or confirm appointees. So exactly what extralegal large-C actions are available to the Congress? Perhaps Congress could claim that its self-help powers should enable it to pass otherwise unconstitutional laws constraining the President's authority in response to a presidential transgression, but the President, of course, would have the power to veto such legislation or seek to avoid its impact through signing statements. Similarly, Congress could attempt to use its contempt powers against the President or her subordinates in a manner that would otherwise be outside its investigation authority, but that action is likely to be futile on the simple grounds that the executive is needed to enforce contempt measures.

To be sure, Congress will still have access to some self-help remedies in the form of its ability to breach any constitutional conventions otherwise constraining its actions. But self-help will vest the President with both that power *and* with meaningful access to extra-legal large-C measures. The extralegal self-help option, in short, adds an immensely powerful weapon to the President's arsenal but comparatively little to the powers of the Congress. It therefore exacerbates the power differential that already exists between the two branches.

In addition, Presidents will likely be particularly aggressive in their use of the self-help power. To begin with, Presidents tend to be forceful in using their authority because of the public expectations that are placed on their performance. The public generally expects the President to act, and her inability to do so is often viewed as failure. Furthermore, Presidents, after they take office, tend to view their agenda as the nation's agenda. They are therefore inclined to view efforts to thwart their agenda as impermissible forms of obstruction that threaten the national interest, justifying retaliation. Third, the availability of self-help would place pressure on an administration to use the remedy even when it otherwise might be reluctant to do so. Saying "no" to one's constituencies becomes more difficult politically when one no longer has the excuse that an action is constitutionally impermissible. Finally, the pressures of legacy will also be in play. Presidents are more commonly judged by what they do than by what they forgo. Given the choice between taking legally uncertain action (of a kind that could be creatively defended as a legitimate use of self-help) or doing nothing, it is difficult to assume that Presidents will commonly pursue the latter option. The siren song enticing the President to make her historical mark is not easily ignored.

The Dangers in Awarding the Presidency the Weapon of Self-Help

Given that the benefits of the self-help remedy will primarily accrue to the President, the question becomes whether that augmentation of presidential power is advisable. The answer, it seems to me, is a clear no. First, as has already been noted, the executive is the most dangerous branch, and its ability to dominate the nation's agenda is unquestioned. Any additions to the President's powers should therefore immediately be deemed suspect.

Second, the self-help remedy is particularly concerning because it is, by definition, a vehicle that trumps constitutional constraints on presidential power. Congress, theoretically, is supposed to be a bulwark against presidential excesses. Self-help, however, comes into play precisely when Congress assumes this blocking function. It also potentially allows a strategic President to turn Congress's checking power on its head. Under a regime of self-help, a President can turn congressional efforts to curb her agenda to her advantage by claiming "obstruction" and then circumventing the Congress by the use of self-help. If there is a theory that better undermines a system of checks and balances, I am not sure what it would be.

Third, the nebulousness surrounding whether the use of self-help is justifiable will also add to the President's power. As some presidential scholars have noted, one of the major reasons why presidential power has already grown so exponentially is that the grant of powers to the President in Article II is so open-ended. This openness allows, and historically has allowed, presidential power to expand when a President asserts that circumstances call for its exercise. A similar dynamic is likely to occur if Pozen's theory of self-help is recognized because the self-help remedy is also extraordinarily open-ended. Determining whether a convention still exists (or has ever existed) will often be a contestable issue, giving the party charged with deciding that issue considerable leeway.

Of course, unlike the powers set forth in Article II, the remedy of self-help is theoretically available to both the Congress and the President. But it is the President, for the reasons discussed in Part II.A, who will be in the better position to take advantage of any ambiguities. That advantage will likely be considerable. After all, as Pozen well recognizes, one of the inherent difficulties in self-help is that the entity charged with determining whether a breach of convention has occurred is the party that is highly motivated to achieve a certain result. And Presidents, as we have already discussed, will be highly motivated.

For this reason, even the requirement that the self-helper's actions must be proportional to the alleged infraction may not prove to be much of a limitation because it will be the self-helper (the President) who will decide the question of proportionality. And there is again little reason to assume the President will be dispassionate in deciding this issue, given that she will often have so much at stake. Therefore, although Pozen's theory strives to guard against egregious excesses in the President's use of self-help by positing that small-c violations by Congress do not justify large-C reactions, the efficacy of that limitation is questionable. After all, the lines between large-C and small-c constitutional violations are not always clear, and even when they are, they appear to be changeable. Presidents, therefore, will have significant ability to capitalize on any ambiguities.

Consider the example that Pozen raises at the outset of his Article—President Obama's unilateral decision to engage in selective enforcement of immigration laws in his Dreamers' initiative in reaction to Republican obstruction of immigration reform. Some would consider the President's selective enforcement action to be a large-C violation (that is, a violation of the Take Care Clause), while the congressional obstruction of immigration reform is at best a small-c infraction if it is any infraction at all. If so, then President Obama acted improperly in promulgating his Dreamers' initiative, even under the terms of self-help, because he reacted to an arguably small-c violation with a large-C response. The problem, of course, is that in the world of self-help, it is only the President's characterization of her and Congress's actions that counts in the initial determination of whether self-help is warranted. So if President Obama concludes that congressional obstruction is either a small-c or large-C violation and that his decision to selectively enforce a statute is either a small-c violation or no violation at all, then his judgment will prevail at least in the short run and most likely in the long term as well (because neither the Court—for reasons of justiciability—nor the Congress—for reasons of collective action—will be able to effectively respond). What empowering the President with self-help does, in effect, is to go a long way towards allowing her to unilaterally draw the boundaries of her own power.

Fourth, the availability of self-help empowers the presidency by allowing it to short-circuit the constraints inherent in the political process. The path of building political consensus across institutions and party lines can be hard and immensely frustrating. The route of claiming that one's opponents are obstreperous is not. When the latter course provides a basis for access to extraordinary powers, it is not difficult to imagine why a President may very quickly give up on the former. Indeed, under a regime of self-help, a strategically motivated President might very well find that her best avenue to achieve a substantive goal is to provoke congressional intransigence so that she, via the remedy of self-help, can achieve a result unfettered by the political compromises that would be necessary if she were to work across party or ideological lines.

Finally, and perhaps most importantly from the long-term perspective in setting the rules of separation of powers, the types of extraordinary actions initially taken under the rubric of self-help could quickly devolve into routine exercises commonly available to the executive. As *Noel Canning* illustrates, the role of precedent is critical in setting both the legal and political legitimacy of subsequent presidential actions. Each time a President exercises a particular power, that action serves both as a legal justification and as political cover for similar exercises of power by her successor. What might be justified as an extraordinary use of a self-help remedy by one President can readily become a routine exercise of power by her successors.

III. Jurisprudential Concerns

Pozen begins his Article by re-characterizing the narrative of President Obama's use of unilateral power from a narrative in which the President has improperly aggrandized his authority to one in which his actions are best understood as reactions to the excesses of Congress. Referring to the President's aggressive use of his recess appointment power and his decisions to selectively enforce immigration laws and the No Child Left Behind Act, Pozen states:

> On one prevalent view, the common thread linking these cases is the disdain they show for constitutional boundaries. The President determines to pursue a legally dubious course of action; he finds executive branch lawyers who will bless his preferred approach; and he forges ahead, heedless of the limits that Congress has placed on him. The episodes, accordingly, "suggest that this president lacks a proper respect for constitutional checks and balances." Abstracting from particulars, they reveal a deep continuity between the Obama Administration and its

predecessors in the contingent, instrumental approach taken to the law when important political objectives are at stake. . . .

[But] another reading of these cases is available, and it points toward a more nuanced conception of the President's relationship to law. On this alternative account, President Obama responded in measured terms to a profound breakdown of the policy process that had come to jeopardize the integrity of representative government. *Congress* was the constitutional villain.

Many, I am sure, would agree with the retelling. Yet at least two other narratives can be imagined. What if, instead of the hyper-partisan obstructionism now taking place, Congress's actions in thwarting the President's legislative initiatives were based on Congress's conclusion that President Obama had violated a constitutional convention by pushing through the Affordable Care Act (ACA) with no bipartisan support? Or what if, more broadly, Congress's obstruction was aimed at remedying the breaches in constitutional conventions committed by prior administrations, in an effort to reverse some of the executive's accretions of power and to regain some semblance of balance between the branches? On these retellings, "improper" constitutional obstruction becomes justifiable congressional self-help.

I raise these hypothetical scenarios because they illustrate some of the jurisprudential and definitional problems inherent in the self-help thesis. First, they demonstrate how inextricably steeped in politics any claims of breach of constitutional convention (or justified self-help response) are likely to be. It is not difficult for politicians to assert they are victims of their opponents' overreaching. The tactic is commonplace. (In fact, many Republicans did argue that the Democrats violated a constitutional convention of sorts when they passed the ACA without bipartisan support.) Accordingly, even if the decision of the legality of a use of self-help could be eventually adjudged by an impartial arbiter rather than left to the discretion of the original self-helper, it would be extraordinarily difficult for that arbiter to develop meaningful standards without immersing itself too far into the "political thicket."

Second, these hypotheticals show how difficult it will be to determine which side engaged in the triggering action that purportedly justifies the self-help response. At which point in the Congress's wrestling with President Obama did one side commit a constitutional wrong: when Senator Mitch McConnell first announced he wanted to limit President Obama to one term, when the Republicans refused to bargain in good faith over the ACA, when the Democrats passed the ACA without bipartisan support, when the Republicans started stalling President Obama's appointments, when the President used recess appointments to fill vacancies on the NLRB, or when the Senate Democrats changed the Senate rules on filibusters to make it easier to confirm the President's nominees? As Pozen himself notes, "[t]here is no value-neutral baseline from which to assess competing charges of constitutional aggrandizement or abdication."

Third, these examples reveal some of the ambiguities (and potential limitlessness) of the self-help claim. Is it for use only by an administration or Congress that has itself been the victim of another branch's alleged wrongdoing? Or does it protect the executive or the Congress more broadly so that each body can use the remedy to redress infractions against their institutions initiated by previous actors? If so, would it be legitimate for Congress to take extra-legal steps of some sort to curtail the executive's war powers during the Obama Administration in response to the aggressive use of those powers by the George W. Bush Administration and by previous administrations? Similarly, would it be legitimate for the Obama Administration to aggressively use its recess appointment powers, claiming that its actions were justified as self-help in response to Congress's acting improperly when some of its Democratic members used filibusters to block President Bush's nominees? Is the self-help remedy, in short, designed to protect institutions against separation of powers transgressions, or is it more individual in the sense that it is meant to protect those particular Congresses and Presidents who can claim that they were improperly aggrieved by the other's actions? Logically, it would seem the remedy should be available for both if its purpose is to correct for institutional wrongdoing. But the problem in viewing self-help in this manner is that it invites both the Congress and the President to take extra-legal actions to correct for infractions going back to the beginning of the federal government. Interbranch grievances are not difficult to find in American history.

Finally, and relatedly, these examples illustrate how the ambiguities inherent in the self-help claim can lead to endless cycles of actions and counteractions coupled with recriminations and counter-recriminations. True, some of this back-and-forth goes on now with each side blaming the other as the cause of the interbranch crisis *du jour*. But whereas now any excesses by one of the branches can be condemned as illegal overreaching, the self-help thesis serves simply as an invitation for more of the same.

IV. A Separation of Powers for All Seasons

Without question, *Self-Help* offers an immensely creative legal solution to some of the gridlock that has currently enveloped the federal government. However, the merits of Pozen's approach need to be evaluated for times when the political dynamics may be far different than they are today. Certainly, the current political climate is poisonous, and any notion that the warring factions are likely to come together any time soon seems at best naive. But it is equally unrealistic to assume that the current state of affairs is the permanent condition. It will not always be true that we will have a relatively weak President facing a highly motivated and intransigent congressional opposition. There will also likely be times when a President may be enormously powerful, and the only thing standing between her and unfettered executive power are a few "obstructionist" members of a congressional minority. Tailoring the separation of powers model to address the particular problems created by the current dysfunction therefore seems misfocused. It is also especially dangerous when the remedy it offers is one that would trump formal constitutional safeguards.

Executive Orders Can Be Checked by Other Branches of Government

Sarah Steers and Mike Roberts

Sarah Steers and Mike Roberts are both attorneys in the Pittsburgh, PA, area.

History of Executive Orders

by Sarah Steers

All but one of the US presidents, beginning with George Washington, have issued orders which can be equated with the modern-day executive order. The sole exception was William Henry Harrison, who died in office after having held the presidency for less than a month. Before 20th century, executive orders were not documented and catalogued according to a uniform scheme; they were seen only by the agencies to which they were directed. Then, in 1907, the Department of State instituted a numbering scheme, starting retroactively with an order dated October 20, 1862, issued by President Abraham Lincoln. The orders which later became known as "executive orders" probably take their name from a document, titled "Executive Order Establishing a Provisional Court in Louisiana."

The Federal Register Act of 1935 required that all executive orders and proclamations be published in the Federal Register. Since then, all executive orders have been made available in CFR Title 3 compilations.

Abraham Lincoln used an executive order to suspend the habeas corpus rights of John Merryman, leader of an active state militia that had been attacking federal troops passing through Virginia and Maryland on the eve of the US Civil War. Later, the US Congress passed the Habeas Corpus Act of 1863, giving the president the power to suspend habeas corpus, which he had assumed himself through the executive order.

"Executive Orders," by Sarah Steers, JURIST Legal News and Research Services, Inc. Reprinted by permission.

There was a dramatic increase in the use of executive orders during the period beginning with the Great Depression and leading into World War II. During this time, Congress extended wide latitude to the president to act in the best interests of a nation facing economic crisis and war. Franklin D. Roosevelt issued, by a wide margin, the largest number of executive orders, with a total of 3,522. He used these orders to seize factories, mines and other privately held assets for wartime production.

To this day, executive orders remain a powerful and immediate way for a president to advance his policies. President Ronald Reagan used executive orders to repeal what his administration viewed as regulations that were holding back the US economy. Notably, President George W. Bush used an executive order to create the Department of Homeland Security. He also used an executive order to limit public access to presidential documents. President Barack Obama has used executive orders to implement policies in the face of what his administration views as an increasingly intractable Congress. He also attempted to use executive orders to change some of President George W. Bush's more controversial policies, including the creation of the detention facility at Guantanamo Bay, which remains open.

Executive Orders and the Supreme Court

by Mike Roberts

Executive orders, like other rules issued by the federal government, are subject to judicial review. A significant example of the Supreme Court striking down a president's executive order came about in 1952. In *Youngstown Sheet & Tube Co. v. Sawyer*, the court held struck down Executive Order 10340, issued by President Harry Truman, which ordered Secretary of Commerce Charles Sawyer to seize control of a majority of the nation's steel mills in anticipation of a steelworker strike during the Korean War. The court held that President Truman lacked the constitutional or statutory power to seize private property.

Following Truman's presidency, the Supreme Court did not invalidate any executive orders for several decades. In *Dames*

& Moore v. Regan, the Court reviewed several executive orders issued by President Reagan which nullified holds on Iranian assets and removed claims against Iran from US courts following the resolution of the Iranian Hostage Crisis. The court took a deferential approach to their review and allowed President Reagan's executive orders to stand. Judicial deference in cases concerning executive orders has largely continued, although a number of executive orders have come under review in district courts.

On July 30, 2014, the US House of Representatives approved a resolution that allowed Speaker John Boehner to sue President Barack Obama over an executive order the president issued altering the timing requirements for implementation of the Affordable Care Act (ACA). The order delayed implementation of certain aspects of the ACA, notably a mandate on employers who did not provide health care coverage. The suit claimed that President Obama's executive powers did not authorize the changing of such a provision. To date, however, the Supreme Court is yet to hear a challenge to any executive order made by President Obama.

Recent Key Executive Orders
by Kyle Webster

Executive Order - Climate-Resilient International Development (not yet numbered) September 23, 2014

This executive order requires that climate-resilience considerations be integrated into all international development work done by all agencies of the United States government, to the fullest legal extent.

Executive Order 13673 - Fair Pay and Safe Workplaces July 31, 2014

This executive order requires potential federal government contractors to disclose labor law violations from the past three years before they can receive a contract and requires that certain agencies designate a "Labor Compliance Advisor." Additionally, federal contractors with $1 million or more in contracts are prohibited from requiring their employees to enter into pre-dispute arbitration agreements for disputes arising out of Title VII or from torts related to sexual assault or harassment. This order permits existing contracts to stay as they currently are.

Executive Order 13672 - Further Amendments to Executive Order 11478, Equal Employment Opportunity in the Federal Government, and Executive Order 11246, Equal Employment Opportunity July 21, 2014

This executive order adds the words "sexual orientation and gender identity" into existing executive orders that prohibit certain forms of discrimination in employment by federal contractors.

Executive Order 13665 - Nonretaliation for Disclosure of Compensation Information April 8, 2014

This executive order prohibits employers working under a government contract from retaliating against employees in regards to their employment for disclosure of compensation information.

Executive Order 13658 - A Minimum Wage for Contractors February 12, 2014

This executive order raises the minimum wage for most federal contractors to $10.10 per hour beginning January 1, 2015. Additionally, beginning January 1, 2016, it empowers the Secretary of Labor to adjust the amount annually.

Additional recent executive orders have dealt with a plethora of issues, including penalizing individuals supporting certain foreign movements in places from South Sudan to Ukraine, expanding the eligibility for the Defense Meritorious Service Medal, and establishing an executive board to review a particular labor dispute.

Do Executive Orders Give the President Too Much Power?

The Separation of Powers According to the Constitution

Goodwin Liu, Pamela S. Karlan, and
Christopher H. Schroeder

Goodwin Liu is Associate Dean and a professor of law at University of California, Berkeley. Pamela S. Karlan is the Kenneth and Harle Montgomery Professor of Public Interest Law at Stanford University. Christopher H. Schroeder is the Charles S. Murphy Professor of Law and a professor of public policy studies at Duke University.

[…]

Separating the powers of the federal government and dividing them among the House and Senate, President, and the Judiciary were decisions fundamental to the Constitution's design. With fresh memories of the Crown's exercise of autocratic authority over the colonies, the Founding generation was determined to prohibit the concentration of government power in the hands of one person or one body. As an "essential precaution in favor of liberty," the Framers created a government that separates the power to make law from the power to execute the law and further separates those powers from the power to try individuals for violating the law. While departing from the Articles of Confederation to create the office of the President, our Constitution conspicuously omits any analog to the dispensing power invoked by British monarchs to disregard acts of Parliament and instead directs the President to "take Care that the Laws be faithfully executed."

In the aftermath of September 11, 2001, President Bush repeatedly claimed that the Constitution gave him authority to act contrary to duly enacted federal statutes. He asserted the right to engage in domestic electronic surveillance despite restrictions

"Keeping Faith with the Constitution," by Goodwin Liu, Pamela S. Karlan, and Christopher H. Schroeder, American Constitution Society for Law and Policy, April 2009. Reprinted by permission.

in the Foreign Intelligence Surveillance Act. He claimed the power to apply so-called enhanced interrogation techniques to persons in US custody despite statutes prohibiting torture. He argued that Congress cannot extend the habeas corpus jurisdiction of federal courts to alien detainees held abroad because it would interfere with the President's authority to conduct the military campaign against al Qaeda. And upon passage of the McCain amendment in 2005 banning cruel, inhuman, or degrading treatment of any person under US custody or control anywhere in the world, President Bush issued a signing statement declaring that he would construe the prohibition subject to his authority as Commander in Chief to protect the nation from further terrorist attacks.

The purported basis for these claims was stated by the Office of Legal Counsel in an August 2002 memorandum examining laws against torture—a memorandum that President Bush's Justice Department subsequently withdrew but whose constitutional reasoning it did not repudiate. "In wartime," the memo stated, "it is for the President alone to decide what methods to use to best prevail against the enemy." The enemy identified by the memo was neither the Taliban in Afghanistan nor the armies of Saddam Hussein in Iraq, but rather "international terrorist organization[s]." Moreover, the Bush administration had previously said the war against terrorism is one that will not end in our lifetimes. Thus, the upshot of reserving to the President alone the authority to decide what methods to use against the enemy would be to grant unfettered discretion to the President, notwithstanding statutory constraints, to pursue any action he believes conducive to interdicting, retaliating against, or gaining intelligence about terrorist activities.

Throughout the world, there are examples of governments led by a strong-man with such unchecked powers. But our nation's Founders made a different choice. A key premise of our Constitution, as James Madison explained, is that "[t]he accumulation of all powers, legislative, executive, and judiciary, in the same hands, whether of one, a few, or many, and whether hereditary, self-appointed, or elective, may justly be pronounced the very definition of tyranny." Our system disperses power among three branches of government—not by making them "wholly unconnected with each other" but by "giv[ing] to each a constitutional control over the others." In other words, ours is a system of checks and balances.

This fundamental principle applies even in times of war. The Founders recognized that the executive must act with dispatch and strength in times of war, but they were deeply concerned about the risk of concentrating too much power in executive hands. The text of the Constitution reflects that concern. It contains seven clauses assigning significant war powers to Congress—the powers to declare war, grant letters of marque and reprisal, and make rules concerning captures on land and water; to raise and support armies; to provide and maintain a navy; to make rules governing land and naval forces; to call forth the militia; to provide for the organizing, arming, and disciplining of the militia; and to define and punish piracies and felonies committed on the high seas and offenses against the law of nations. By contrast, the war powers committed to the President derive solely from his designation as Commander in Chief of the armed forces and the militia.

In times of emergency, the President is naturally inclined toward robust action in the nation's defense, and the Commander in Chief authority ensures unified control of our armed forces. While reserving to Congress the power to declare war, the Founders certainly expected the President to have the power to repel sudden attacks without prior congressional authorization. Such power is meant to authorize the President not to create a state of war but to use force to defend the nation when conditions of exigency make prior approval by Congress impractical and when the President reasonably anticipates that Congress will support the action after the fact. But nothing in the Constitution's text or framing history suggests that the President's power to repel sudden attacks displaces

Congress's authority under its war powers (or other powers) to make law that is binding on the executive after the emergency has passed.

In recent years, the most aggressive claims of executive authority have relied not on the well-established power to respond to exigencies but instead on the President's prerogative as Commander in Chief to make strategic and tactical decisions in wartime. As the August 2002 memorandum by the Office of Legal Counsel put it, "Congress lacks authority under Article I to set the terms and conditions under which the President may exercise his authority as Commander-in-Chief to control the conduct of operations during a war." Under this theory, "Congress may no more regulate the President's ability to detain and interrogate enemy combatants than it may regulate his ability to direct troop movements on the battlefield." And so, "[j]ust as statutes that order the President to conduct warfare in a certain manner or for specific goals would be unconstitutional, so too are laws that seek to prevent the President from gaining the intelligence he believes necessary to prevent attacks upon the United States."

These assertions go beyond the claim that the President has inherent power to conduct military operations in the nation's defense absent congressional authorization. The latter claim is an interpretation of presidential power within what Justice Jackson called the "zone of twilight," where the "absence of either a congressional grant or denial of authority" invites the President to "rely upon his own independent powers" even as "he and Congress may have concurrent authority, or . . . its distribution is uncertain." Justice Jackson recognized that presidential claims of inherent power in this zone of twilight (Category Two in his tripartite analytical framework) are often controversial, with "any actual test of power . . . likely to depend on the imperatives of events and contemporary imponderables rather than on abstract theories of law." Even more controversial, then, are Category Three cases—such as the recent examples above—where the President claims "preclusive" power to "take[] measures incompatible with the expressed or implied will of Congress." Here the President's power "is at its lowest ebb." Such claims of executive authority "must be scrutinized with caution" lest they undermine "the equilibrium established by our constitutional system."

Throughout our nation's history, the equilibrium to which Justice Jackson referred is one that has eschewed any broad assignment of preclusive power to the President in his role as Commander in Chief. Textually, the Constitution's designation of the President as Commander in Chief does suggest some limits on congressional control. For example, Congress may not alter the military hierarchy by assigning ultimate command of the armed forces to a military officer or to anyone other than the President. Nor may Congress delegate responsibility for the conduct of a military campaign to an officer insulated from presidential direction or removal. These limitations marked a significant change from the power that the Articles of Confederation had given to Congress to appoint officers of the armed forces.

It is far less clear, however, that the President's authority as Commander in Chief precludes congressional enactments that substantively direct the conduct of military campaigns. In an exhaustive survey of evidence from Founding-era practices, the constitutional convention, and the state ratification process, David Barron and Martin Lederman conclude that historically "the legislature possessed the power to subject the executive to control over all matters pertaining to warmaking," including "such clearly tactical matters as the movement of troops." "[N]otwithstanding recent attempts to yoke the defense of executive defiance in wartime to original understandings," they explain, "there is surprisingly little Founding-era evidence supporting the notion that the conduct of military campaigns is beyond legislative control and a fair amount of evidence that affirmatively undermines it."

During the Revolutionary War, for example, the Continental Congress exercised extensive authority over the strategies and tactics, including troop deployments, ordered by George Washington as commander in chief of the colonial army.

Scrupulously deferential to congressional dictates, Washington never assumed that he had authority to disobey a legislative command, even when he believed Congress's judgment to be clearly wrong. Similarly, there is no indication in early state constitutions that the commander in chief of the militia could act contrary to statutes governing military affairs. The constitutions of several states, including Massachusetts and New Hampshire, made clear that the war powers of the commander in chief were subject to legislative control.

If we look beyond original understandings, we find little evidence in our constitutional practice of any widely shared understanding that the President's authority as Commander in Chief precludes congressional regulation of military operations. even during the Civil War, a reference point often invoked by contemporary defenders of robust executive power, "Lincoln himself never once asserted a broad power to disregard statutory limits, not even during his well-known exercise of expansive executive war powers at the onset of hostilities or when confronted with statutes that challenged his own tactical choices later in the war." In particular, when President Lincoln in April 1861 authorized his generals to suspend habeas corpus in response to rioting in various states, he defended his action on two grounds: first, that the suspension was a necessary response to a genuine emergency at a time when Congress was not in session, and second, that the Article I Suspension Clause empowers the President, in Congress's absence, to suspend habeas corpus when the nation faces rebellion. Whatever the merits of these arguments, they were "a far cry from a claim of general power pursuant to the Commander in Chief Clause to defy statutes regulating the conduct of war." Indeed, President Lincoln conceded that the suspension was subject to congressional override, and when Congress passed the Habeas Corpus Act of 1863 limiting the President's suspension power, neither he nor his administration argued that the statute would be unconstitutional if it constrained the President's detention policies during war.

Equally relevant is President Lincoln's acquiescence to the

confiscation act that Congress passed in 1862. Despite his concern that seizing rebel property and emancipating certain slaves as tactics for ending the war risked alienating the border states, "no executive branch official—including the President and his Attorney General—contended at any point in the extensive debate that the Act unconstitutionally interfered with the President's constitutional war authority" even though that argument had been thoroughly aired in Congress.

The history of our constitutional practice reveals no longstanding tradition of preclusive executive power to control the conduct of war, although the claim has surfaced more often since the mid-twentieth century. President Truman invoked preclusive as well as inherent power as Commander in Chief in deploying forces to Europe in 1951 to counter the Soviet threat, but it does not appear that the deployment actually violated any federal statutes. And while many believe Truman exceeded his inherent powers when he committed troops to the Korean War without prior congressional authorization, his action did not rely on preclusive power to disregard a statutory prohibition. Over the next fifty years, Congress passed numerous laws restricting the President's power to conduct military operations, including legislation in 1971 prohibiting US deployment of ground troops in Cambodia, the War Powers Resolution in 1973, the Foreign Intelligence Surveillance Act in 1978, and the Boland Amendments in the 1980s restricting military aid to the Contras in Nicaragua. Although nearly all of President Truman's successors claimed preclusive power in one or more circumstances, the practice was not consistent and often left unclear whether the claim was made in anticipation of future circumstances or in response to an applicable law on the books. "Certainly there was no sustained practice of actually disregarding statutes similar to that we have seen since September 11, 2001." Further, it is worth noting that, from the Founding to the present day, the Supreme Court has never invalidated a federal statute on the ground that it improperly interfered with the President's constitutional prerogative to conduct a military campaign.

Faced with this history, recent defenders of preclusive presidential power have argued that new constitutional understandings are required in order to meet new threats to national security. The principal author of the Office of Legal Counsel's August 2002 memorandum on torture has explained that traditional checks and balances "might have been more appropriate at the end of the Cold War, when conventional warfare between nation-states remained the chief focus of concern and few threats seemed to challenge American national security." Today, however, "it certainly is no longer clear that the constitutional system ought to be fixed so as to make it difficult to use force" given the emergence of rogue nations, the easy availability of weapons of mass destruction, and the rise of international terrorism. Instead of maintaining "a warmaking system that place[s] a premium on consensus, time for deliberation, and the approval of multiple institutions," the argument goes, now "[t]he United States must have the option to use force earlier and more quickly than in the past."

Although arguments for preclusive power based on societal change can hold no sway among those who believe in an originalism of expected applications, they nonetheless merit careful consideration because our Constitution's text and principles were meant to be adapted to new challenges and not frozen in time. In the war on terrorism, we face an asymmetrical conflict where the enemy is not a nation-state but a diffuse and hidden network, where enemy tactics include the targeting of civilian populations, where armed struggle is not confined to a traditional battlefield, and where the enemy's sources of financing and support are largely secret and not rooted in a territorial homeland. These conditions differ in many ways from past conflicts with nation-states that have agreed to abide by laws of war, and the unconventional nature of the enemy and its tactics may call for novel responses. The question is whether effective responses to terrorist threats require an allocation of decision-making authority that departs from original understandings of separation of powers and its actual practice throughout our history—in particular, the longstanding power of Congress to regulate the President's conduct of military campaigns.

It may be too soon to answer the question definitively, given the recency of the war on terrorism. But the argument for unchecked presidential power based on changed conditions should be viewed with great skepticism. As an initial matter, we ought not assume too quickly that the threat of terrorism is entirely different from security threats that our nation has confronted in the past. "The United States has long been troubled by sub-state actors engaged in non-traditional tactics to undermine US interests," beginning with the Barbary pirates during the Founding era. But even acknowledging the important differences between today's threats and those of the past, it is not obvious that effective responses require an enlargement of presidential power up to and including the power to disregard federal statutes constraining the exercise of executive war powers.

As a functional matter, our nation's "history undermines assertions about the inherent or inevitable unmanageability or dangers of recognizing legislative control over the conduct of war." In the war on terrorism, there is little evidence so far to suggest that complying with existing laws or engaging Congress in passing new legislation has hampered the President's prosecution of the war. Where the President has asked Congress for greater authority, Congress has generally been willing to provide it.

For example, after the National Security Agency's secret warrantless surveillance program came to light in 2005, the Attorney General argued that the program was a proper exercise of the President's power as Commander in Chief because existing statutory authority for government wiretapping was inadequate to meet national security needs. The secret program was justified, the Attorney General claimed, despite procedures in the Foreign Intelligence Surveillance Act that comprised "the exclusive means" for conducting domestic electronic surveillance. The President, however, had never asked Congress for additional authority. Once the national security needs were made clear to Congress, legislators enacted the authorizations necessary to put the surveillance within a legal framework that balances effective intelligence-gathering with important privacy concerns.

Notably, the Supreme Court has shown no inclination to endorse claims of preclusive power in the war on terrorism. Every major decision by the Court in this area has invoked traditional understandings of checks and balances. In *Rasul v. Bush,* for example, the Court held that federal courts have jurisdiction under the federal habeas statute to hear suits by Guantánamo detainees challenging the legality of their detention, effectively rejecting the President's argument that reading the habeas statute this way would unconstitutionally interfere with his Commander in Chief power.

Similarly, in *Hamdi v. Rumsfeld,* the President claimed "plenary authority" to detain indefinitely an American citizen captured as an enemy combatant in Afghanistan despite a federal statute prohibiting the detention of citizens. In a plurality opinion joined by Chief Justice Rehnquist, Justice Kennedy, and Justice Breyer, Justice O'Connor declined to reach the President's broad claim, instead upholding the detention on the ground that the Authorization of the Use of Military Force enacted by Congress after September 11, 2001, provided sufficient authorization for the detention. Rather than endorse a broad construction of the Commander in Chief power, the plurality situated the President's action within the confines of a duly enacted statute. Further, the plurality elaborated the due process requirements applicable to the detention. In doing so, Justice O'Connor reaffirmed our settled understanding of separation of powers:

> [The President's argument] serves only to condense power into
> a single branch of government. We have long since made clear
> that a state of war is not a blank check for the President when
> it comes to the rights of the Nation's citizens. Whatever power
> the United States Constitution envisions for the executive in its
> exchanges with other nations or with enemy organizations in
> times of conflict, it most assuredly envisions a role for all three

branches when individual liberties are at stake.

Subsequently, the Court in *Hamdan v. Rumsfeld* held that military tribunals created by President Bush purportedly through his inherent power as Commander in Chief were not authorized by statute and violated the Uniform Code of Military Justice and the Geneva Conventions. In reaching its holding, the Court rejected the notion of preclusive presidential power by saying: "Whether or not the President has independent power, absent congressional authorization, to convene military commissions, he may not disregard limitations that Congress has, in proper exercise of its own war powers, placed on his powers." As Justice Breyer observed, "[n]othing prevents the President from returning to Congress to seek the authority he believes necessary." After *Hamdan,* the President did precisely that, and Congress responded by enacting legislation authorizing military commissions for aliens detained as enemy combatants.

Although it is fair to say that the statutes examined in *Rasul, Hamdi,* and *Hamdan* are not models of legislative clarity or foresight, the decisions in those cases ultimately reflect the Court's adherence to Justice Jackson's dictum that "[w]ith all its defects, delays and inconveniences, men have discovered no technique for long preserving free government except that the executive be under the law, and that the law be made by parliamentary deliberations." Neither original understandings nor the lessons of constitutional practice, including our most recent experiences in the war on terrorism, provide reason to question that wisdom. In sum, fidelity to the Constitution requires that we preserve, not abandon, the core principle of checks and balances by working within our system of divided power to meet new challenges through democratic means.

[…]

Executive Orders Can Have Long-Term Negative Effects

Nathan Hultman

Dr. Nathan Hultman is Director of the Center for Global Sustainability and an associate professor at the University of Maryland School of Public Policy.

Today the White House issued an executive order on domestic energy policy that seeks to hobble or reverse some of broad set of climate and clean energy initiatives developed by the Obama administration, including an important component called the Clean Power Plan that would reduce emissions from electricity generation.

First and most prominently, the executive order directs the Environmental Protection Agency to review the Clean Power Plan, one of Obama's key regulatory actions to drive down greenhouse gas emissions in the electric power sector. Because an executive order cannot directly overturn a regulation, the EPA will have to come to a finding about whether the CPP should be revised or repealed. Technically, the EPA does not have an option to repeal and not replace, because the Supreme Court has already ruled that the current interpretation of the Clean Air Act—the legislation upon which the CPP is based—requires the EPA to regulate carbon dioxide as a pollutant. Repeal without replacement would contravene the Supreme Court's order, so Trump's EPA must come up with an alternative that will hold up in court.

While determining the fate of the CPP will end up being an immensely complex multi-year undertaking, the order also includes the following actions that can be carried out quickly:

- Reversing Obama's moratorium on new coal mining leases on federal lands;

"Trump's Executive Order on Energy Independence," by Nathan Hultman, Brookings Institute, March 28, 2017. Reprinted by permission.

- Removing the consideration of greenhouse gases from permit reviews under the National Environmental Policy Act;
- Formally abandoning Obama's roadmap on how to achieve US emissions reductions
- Eliminating a tool for cost-benefit analysis in regulatory review called the "Social Cost of Carbon"

So what are the implications for former President Obama's climate plans and, more broadly, the overall trajectory of US greenhouse gas emissions?

First, dismantling the CPP would put the US on a higher pollution and less ambitious emissions track in the medium term. The CPP targeted a roughly 32 percent decrease in CO_2 emissions from the power sector by 2030, primarily from accelerating the long-term shift away from coal-fired electricity generation. In addition to having impacts on the US economy and health, removing the CPP would imply a costly delay in implementing what in the long run will be necessary reductions in our overall greenhouse gas emissions over time. In addition, the approach in the CPP was developed over many years of consultation with industry, health advocates, states, and other stakeholders. While it would impact coal, it did provide a reasonable approach to reducing the most harmful emissions and steering the economy toward a sounder energy system for the future.

The EPA had previously estimated substantial benefits from the CPP, including $14–34 billion in benefits accruing just to health, with 3,600 premature deaths, 1,700 heart attacks, 90,000 asthma attacks, and of 300,000 lost work and school days avoided *every year*. These are significant impacts that Trump's EPA will have to justify abandoning—both to constituents and to the courts.

In addition, while Trump argues that the CPP rollback will benefit jobs, he is referring to a relatively small set of interests. While it is important to be mindful of the need to blunt the potential economic hardship that people working in dying industries face, even insiders acknowledge that the coal sector is not going to recover even with these rules rolled back, not least because of mechanization. Recent Department of Energy statistics show that the coal mining industry employed roughly 66,000 miners in 2015, compared to an estimated 3 million jobs supported by clean energy. Therefore, the likely impact of the order on the coal industry will be fairly weak in the near term and, at best, mediocre in the long term. While reversing the moratorium on new coal mining leases will open new sources of supply, it will not in itself reverse the trends in energy markets that have increasingly favored gas. In addition, other regulations to control air pollution will continue to restrict the burning of coal for electricity.

In short, there are better ways to encourage work for those disaffected by the shifting of tectonic plates of the energy economy.

Moreover, removing the regulations may not produce any net jobs, and could in fact cause a net decrease in jobs in the long run. Jobs projections are always somewhat uncertain, and in any jobs comparison, it's important to think of the economy as a whole. In other words, if we are producing less electricity from new technologies like wind and solar—industries that also promote energy self-sufficiency and reduce US reliance on foreign sources—we are actually hurting job growth in those industries. Given the long-term pressures to increase clean energy globally— which will not go away just because Trump chooses to ignore them—hobbling our innovative clean energy industry in pursuit of a fleeting last gasp for polluting, 19th century technology is a terrible economic strategy, even aside from the health, economic, and environmental damage that increased coal use will cause.

Removing and replacing the CPP would entail a long, arduous process, and Trump's path is fraught with obstacles. Even if the EPA tries to move forward with an alternate regulation, or just chooses to ignore existing regulations, the EPA is currently legally obligated to regulate CO_2. Since the Supreme Court has ruled that CO_2 is a pollutant under the Clean Air Act, if EPA chooses not to regulate CO_2, it will be sued.

In some ways, Trump has a parallel political problem to the one he faced on health care: finding a solution that satisfies the most strident coal advocates while balancing broader concerns about health and broad-based support for other, cleaner sources of energy. Even if Trump prevails, doing so will create costs for him and vulnerabilities for Republican representatives who will face angry constituents concerned, among other things, about respiratory health, climate change, and cleaner energy.

Dismantling the CPP would have an effect on the overall US climate strategy and will make it harder and more expensive to achieve the necessary levels of greenhouse gas emissions in the longer term. But it is also important to remember that the CPP, in targeting roughly one-third of overall US greenhouse gas emissions, is only one part of the overall strategy to drive down US emissions. Electricity currently makes up about 39 percent of US energy use and is responsible for about 30 percent of overall US greenhouse gas emissions. While many of the most inexpensive and economically efficient opportunities for emissions reductions exist in the power sector, a number of other areas that will continue to see efficiency gains, such as in appliance and equipment standards and the first round of auto fuel economy standards implemented under Obama. As one example, existing appliance and equipment efficiency standards are expected to reduce US CO_2 emissions by 3 billion tons by 2030—fully half of the estimated reductions from the CPP.

Within the United States, broader market forces will continue to advance cleaner energy supply and efficiency technologies. Unlike large fossil fuel generation, clean energy technologies tend to become rapidly cheaper over time. In the past eight years, we have seen costs for wind drop by 40 percent, solar by over 60 percent, and energy-saving LED lights by 90 percent. In many places, clean energy is now, and will remain, cost-competitive as technology costs drop. While these trends alone will not be able to keep the US on a trajectory to avoid the most dangerous effects of climate change, they bolster the case that clean energy is an attractive, innovation-oriented growth option for our economy, and one that undoubtedly many stakeholders will be pressing for in the months ahead and in future elections.

Finally, although Trump's directive does not directly address American engagement in the Paris Agreement or other international climate agreements, it does have some implications for broader US engagement in international climate policy. Rolling back the CPP would remove an important component of the American climate strategy and make it more difficult to achieve longer-term US climate targets. Other players, including big emitters like China, the European Union, and India, are aware of Trump's stance on climate and will not be surprised by this action: most countries have committed to continuing to pursue their own climate goals, in part because they view doing so as good for their own domestic politics and economies. Nevertheless, such a retreat from responsibility by the world's second-largest emitter of greenhouse gases represents an obstacle to the ambitious global goals for climate stabilization set out in recent years. While it is possible that some countries may in turn weaken their own ambition as a result, so far it appears that many have decided to continue to push forward. Nevertheless, the long-term success of the global approach to climate change, based on the Paris Agreement, depends on continued broad engagement to encourage a cycle of positive action. Trump's approach threatens to break this cycle. Continued engagement by states and other actors, and a near-term re-engagement by the US, will be important to bolster global ambition to tackle this challenge.

President Trump's Executive Order Will Contribute to Climate Change

Marianne Lavelle

Marianne Lavelle is a reporter for Inside Climate News. *She has covered environment, science, law, and business in Washington, DC, for more than two decades.*

President Donald Trump signed an executive order on Tuesday calling on every federal agency to loosen the regulatory reins on fossil fuel industries, the most significant declaration of the administration's intent to retreat from action on climate change.

Trump directed all departments to identify and target for elimination any rules that restrict US production of energy, and he set guidance to make it more difficult to put future regulations in place on the coal, oil and natural gas industries.

The White House sought to frame the Executive Order on Promoting Energy Independence and Economic Growth as an "all-of-the-above" energy policy. "We're looking at deposits of coal, looking at nuclear, looking at renewables, all of it," said a senior administration official in a briefing. But the primary aim is clearly to unleash fossil fuel development by undoing the policies that President Barack Obama put in place to curb the nation's carbon emissions.

Trump's executive order steered clear of whether the US will remain a party to the Paris climate agreement. The White House has not yet made a decision, the official said. But gutting climate policies as the executive order seeks to do would make the US obligations under the treaty virtually impossible to meet. It would also put in jeopardy the landmark agreement's goal of keeping the global temperature increase below 2 degrees Celsius.

Trump specifically ordered the Environmental Protection Agency to initiate a review of the Clean Power Plan, the Obama

"Trump's Executive Order: More Fossil Fuels, Regardless of Climate Change," by Marianne Lavelle, *Inside Climate News*, March 28, 2017. Reprinted by permission.

administration's signature climate initiative to slash carbon pollution from coal plants. The process of repealing that regulation, which is currently under a stay by the Supreme Court, could take years. But even as that battle wends its way through the process, Trump's order will have a potentially sweeping impact by immediately rescinding a series of Obama executive orders that embedded consideration of climate change into all major decisions by the federal government.

"Those orders have already kind of run their course," said the administration official, who spoke on the condition of anonymity because he was discussing the order before its formal release. "They don't reflect the president's priorities when it comes to dealing with climate change. We want to do it with our own policy, in our own fashion."

That policy, in essence, is to produce more energy, regardless of carbon emissions. "No. 1, you've got to make sure you've got a strong economy," the official said. "A strong economy is the best way to protect the environment. Natural gas is important. Coal is important. Nuclear is important."

The executive order did not address the Environmental Protection Agency's endangerment finding—the Obama administration's declaration in 2009 that carbon dioxide and other greenhouse gases constitute a threat to ecosystems and public health. That finding, which a federal appeals court in 2012 said was "unambiguously correct," is the legal underpinning of the EPA acting to address climate change under the Clean Air Act. The senior White House official expressed a view, not widely shared, that the endangerment finding only applied to vehicle regulations and did not give the EPA an obligation to address carbon emissions from power plants under a different section of the law. (Supreme Court rulings in 2011 and 2014 further cemented EPA's authority to use the Clean Air Act to address power plant pollution.)

Trump signed the order with great fanfare, in front of a group of about a dozen coal miners, at the EPA headquarters, and flanked by Vice President Mike Pence, EPA Administrator Scott Pruitt and his secretaries of energy and interior.

"This is the start of a new era in American energy production and job creation," Trump said. "We will eliminate federal overreach, restore economic freedom and allow workers and companies to play on a level playing field for the first time in a long time, a long time.

"We're going to have clean coal, really clean coal."

Trump and his cabinet members made no mention of climate change as they made their remarks, nor did they talk about nuclear energy or renewables, as the White House official did the previous day in briefing reporters on the planned order. Instead, they framed the order as a job-creating, economic stimulus measure, turning repeatedly to the coal miners behind them on stage as they extolled its benefits. "You know what this says?" Trump asked them. "This says you're going back to work."

The repeal of US climate policy efforts is sure to fire up environmental activists and scientists who gathered in protest outside EPA headquarters and were planning a rally in front of the White House later in the day. They are also organizing two significant marches on Washington, D.C. in late April.

Activists hope the People's Climate March set for April 29 recreates their success in bringing 400,000 people into the streets of New York during the United Nations General Assembly in 2014. Scientists are also organizing a March for Science on April 22, which is Earth Day.

"This is an all-out assault on the protections we need to avert climate catastrophe," said Rhea Suh, president of the Natural Resources Defense Council. "It's a senseless betrayal of our national interests. And it's a short-sighted attempt to undermine American clean energy leadership."

Still, the order did not go far enough to please some of Trump's supporters, including Myron Ebell, of the conservative Competitive Enterprise Institute and Trump's EPA transition leader, who supports a US withdrawal from the Paris accord and action to rescind the endangerment finding. "It is important to understand that all these policies are closely connected and that striking down most but not all of them will not be sufficient to undo the damage done by President Obama's energy-rationing policies," Ebell said.

The Trump order eliminates guidance that Obama's Council on Environmental Quality issued last August on how agencies should incorporate climate considerations into the environmental reviews they are required to conduct on all major federal actions under the National Environmental Policy Act (NEPA.) The State Department's NEPA review of the Keystone XL pipeline, for example, considered the project's impact on greenhouse gases. The analysis became the basis of Obama's decision to kill the project that would move Canadian tar sands oil to refineries in the United States. (Trump revived the Keystone XL by granting the project a presidential permit last week.)

But Trump could face legal challenges if agencies begin producing NEPA reviews without taking climate change into account. Courts have invalidated rules for failure to consider it as part of an environmental review, legal experts said.

Jessica Wentz, associate director of the Sabin Center for Climate Change Law at Columbia University, believes the only way federal agencies could legally ignore climate change would be for Congress to rewrite the 1969 NEPA law. "While they weren't explicitly thinking about climate change, it is broadly worded and talks of reserving resources for future generations," she said. "It makes perfect sense to apply it to the biggest environmental threat to the planet now."

Trump's order also directs a reconsideration of the government's use of the "social cost of carbon," a measurement that puts a price on the future damage society will pay for every ton of carbon dioxide emitted. Federal agencies are required by law to weigh the costs and benefits of most regulations, and the social cost of carbon has become an important tool for tallying the risks of business as usual on global warming. Yale environmental economist William Nordhaus recently wrote that it was "the most important single economic concept in the economics of climate change."

The executive order did not simply scrap the social-cost calculations because the White House likely realized such a blunt approach would not pass legal muster. A federal appeals court in 2007 threw out Bush administration fuel economy standards for SUVs for failure to account for the cost of greenhouse gas emissions.

Instead, the White House ordered agencies to use calculation methods developed by its budget office 14 years ago for decisions not involving greenhouse gas emissions. The result will be a new metric for the social damage costs that sets the number far lower.

"This gets down to a question of whether we value the here and now and not what happens to future generations," said Chris Forest, an atmospheric scientist at Pennsylvania State University.

Trump's order also requires a review of a 2015 EPA regulation for new fossil fuel power plants to be built with carbon-control technologies. (The Clean Power Plan applies to existing power plants.) The new measure also demands review of an EPA regulation finalized last May to monitor and control methane leaks at new oil and gas facilities.

As expected, the new order lifted the moratorium on new coal mining leases on federal lands that Obama put in place a year ago. Obama had directed the Interior Department to determine whether to charge companies higher leasing and royalty fees for mining public lands coal, in part to reflect the climate costs associated with emissions from the coal. Lifting the moratorium is expected to have little immediate impact, because production has continued on current federal leases, which already can provide ample coal for decades. And due to the slump in demand for coal, production in Wyoming and Montana, where most of those leases would be sold, fell 18 percent in 2016. Cheap natural gas and renewable energy have beaten back coal's share of US electricity generation, a trend that Trump will find it difficult to reverse.

On Wednesday, Interior Secretary Ryan Zinke signed the paperwork: one order to overturn the leasing moratorium and to end a broad environmental impact assessment, and another to reexamine climate change guidance and policies across the agency.

He also chartered a new panel to advise him on how much companies should pay for the public land coal reserves they mine and sell.

Many Congressional Republicans and industry groups praised Trump's executive order.

"For eight years President Obama waged an all-out war on fossil fuels and pushed a relentless agenda to regulate carbon dioxide," said Sen. James Inhofe (R-Okla.), one of Congress' leading opponents of climate action. "This slowed our economy drastically and damaged our national security by limiting our ability to use affordable, domestically sourced energy."

Scott Segal, director of the Electric Reliability Coordinating Council, a group of power-generating companies, said the order will help Trump in his oft-stated goal of spurring pipelines, transmission projects, and other energy infrastructure. "It is possible to have an effective climate change policy based more on market principles than command and control regulations," Segal said.

The order set off criticism from Democrats and environmental advocates, who said that the Trump administration would set back progress on clean air and water, while failing to address the woes of workers who have been hurt by the demise of the coal industry. While market forces and increasing automation will continue to make mining jobs scarce, the Trump administration's policy would ensure those communities lose out on the opportunities that clean energy technologies could provide, they said.

"The administration's 'Back to the Future' environmental policy might be funny if it were a movie, but it's real life," said Gina McCarthy, who shepherded the Clean Power Plan as Obama's EPA administrator. "They want us to travel back to when smokestacks damaged our health and polluted our air, instead of taking every opportunity to support clean jobs of the future. This is not just dangerous; it's embarrassing to us and our businesses on a global scale to be dismissing opportunities for new technologies, economic growth, and US leadership."

Congress Can Take Action to Prevent the Abuse of Executive Orders

Todd Gaziano

Todd Gaziano is Executive Director of Pacific Legal Foundation's Washington, DC Center and Senior Fellow in Constitutional Law. He has served in all three branches of the federal government and is a well-known scholar and leader in the liberty legal movement.

For the record, I am a Senior Fellow in Legal Studies and Director of the Center for Legal and Judicial Studies at The Heritage Foundation, an independent research and educational organization. I am a graduate of the University of Chicago Law School and a former law clerk to the US Fifth Circuit Court of Appeals. I also served in the US Department of Justice, Office of Legal Counsel, during different periods in the Reagan, Bush, and Clinton Administrations, where I provided constitutional advice to the White House and four Attorneys General. Several years ago, I also was privileged to serve as chief counsel for another Subcommittee of this House.

[…]

In my oral testimony, I would like to focus on two somewhat distinct areas. The first is the general constitutional framework for executive directives. The second is what Congress can do to reassert its prerogatives and make sure that the President does not usurp them.

The Separation of Powers

One of the great and enduring gifts from the Founders' generation was the inclusion of separation of power principles in the United States Constitution. The Framers had studied the writings of Montesquieu and other political philosophers as well as the

"Executive Orders and Presidential Directives," by Todd Gaziano, Heritage Foundation, March 22, 2001. Reprinted by permission.

workings of the separate branches of their own state governments. Their conscious design to enforce this separation of functions was carefully explained in *The Federalist Papers* and during the debates over ratification of the United States Constitution. The separation of powers is now enshrined in both the structure of the Constitution and various explicit provisions of Articles I, II, and III.

Yet, in the previous Administration, a baser motive seemed to prevail in the use of executive power. Former President Bill Clinton proudly publicized his use of executive decrees in situations where he failed to achieve a legislative objective. Moreover, he repeatedly flaunted his executive order power to curry favor with narrow or partisan special interests. History will show that President Clinton abused his authority in a variety of ways and that his disrespect for the rule of law was unprecedented. Given this pattern, no one should be surprised that President Clinton sometimes abused his executive order authority as well.

A President who abuses his executive order authority undermines the constitutional separation of powers and may even violate it. But the constitutional separation of powers supports both sides of the argument over a President's proper authority. It reinforces a President's right or duty to issue a decree, order, or proclamation to carry out a particular power that truly is committed to his discretion by the Constitution or by a lawful statute passed by Congress. On the other hand, the constitutional separation of powers cuts the other way if the President attempts to issue an order regarding a matter that is expressly committed to another branch of government; it might even render the presidential action void. Finally, separation of powers principles may be unclear or ambiguous when the power is shared by two branches of government.

Thus, no simple recitation of governing law or prudential guidelines is possible. However, history and practice are useful tools in understanding the President's authority, and a legal framework of analysis exists to help determine issues of validity. In addition to the information in our memorandum, I would be happy to answer the Members' questions on these matters.

Recommendations for Congress

In the attached Heritage *Legal Memorandum*, we provided our thoughts on some priorities for the current President to correct the errors and abuses of the previous President in five issue areas: foreign and defense policy, environmental policy, regulatory review, labor policy, and civil rights. For example, President Clinton's land designations under the Antiquities Act were improper and many, if not most, were probably illegal. We opined that the President probably could rescind those that were improper. In addition, he can change the boundaries of the monuments, significantly reduce the acreage involved, and alter the restrictions for portions of the monument lands.

Whether some of these lands should be protected or not, it would be best in my view if President Bush rescinded the monument designations with a message to Congress that he would be happy to sign legislation that Congress sent to him regarding such lands. That said, it is probably not the best use of the Subcommittee's time to hear me talk about what I think a different branch of government should do, whether it is the executive branch or the courts. Regardless of what President Bush does to restore faith in the Office of the President—and I think President Bush has taken some very positive steps in the area of executive orders—Congress should take the following steps to prevent future abuses and protect its prerogatives:

First, Congress should modify or repeal the statutory delegations of power that Congress has granted to the President which have been abused or may be abused in the future. Let me stress that I have no reason to suspect that President Bush would abuse his authority. He has shown every indication that his example will be a good one. Yet, this very fact suggests there is a satisfactory basis for Congress to work with the executive branch to review some of these grants of authority and reach an agreement on possible legislative changes.

For example, Congress did not significantly amend the Antiquities Act of 1906 when it revised many land management laws during the 1970s. Presidents Ford, Reagan, and George H.W. Bush did not make any monument designations under the Antiquities Act, but Presidents Carter and Clinton abused their authority to remove millions of acres of land from public use. Thus, I would recommend that Congress revise the type of land that can be designated as a monument under the Antiquities Act. More importantly, however, I think Congress should tighten up the language that requires monuments to be "the smallest area compatible with the proper care and management of the objects to be protected." Because some Presidents have shown no intention of being limited by such descriptive words, I also recommend that Congress limit the amount of land that can be designated under the Antiquities Act without additional statutory authority to something like 5,000 acres.

The President could seek a waiver from such an acreage limitation if it were necessary, and there are other laws that can be used to designate national parks, wild and scenic waters, etc. But it is unclear to me why Congress would want the President to have unilateral power to lock away tens of millions of acres of land as a national monument, but it would not grant the President equivalent authority to make the same land a national reserve or park. Consistency may be the hobgoblin of little minds, but it should not be dismissed out of hand when someone points out that it is lacking.

The International Emergency Economic Powers Act (IEEPA) was intended to limit the President's emergency powers during peace time. The era since IEEPA's passage has witnessed an improvement upon earlier abuses, but IEEPA has still spawned "multiple concurrent states of national emergency," to quote one scholar. Although some of the authority granted to the President may be necessary in a true national emergency, I believe Congress should reassess the standards and threshold for a declaration of national emergency in that Act.

A second step Congress can take is further consideration of some of the process reforms contained in such bills as H.R. 2655, the Separation of Powers Restoration Act, which was introduced in the last Congress by Representatives Ron Paul (R-TX) and Jack Metcalf (R-WA). H.R. 2655 would have required that all presidential directives specify the constitutional and statutory basis for any action incorporated in the directive or be void as to parties outside the executive branch. With few exceptions, most recent Presidents before Clinton did cite the font of their authority in their executive directives. President Clinton cited some authority in a majority of his directives, but others were vague or had no citation of authority at all. A faithful executive should not have a problem citing the authority for his actions, and this requirement would help citizens, lawyers, and the courts evaluate new directives. Although there may be some constitutional problems with the application of this requirement in some cases, it is worth further consideration and possible refinement.

H.R. 2655 also would have attempted to expand the number of parties with standing to challenge an arguably unlawful directive, including Members of Congress, state and local officials, and any aggrieved person. Because part of the standing doctrine is constitutional, a statute could not automatically confer standing on someone without a "particularized" injury in fact. Nevertheless, the provision would potentially expand the range and number of persons who could bring suit to challenge a questionable directive by removing any statutory impediments to suit.

Finally, I think Congress should encourage the President to institute internal reforms, including those that are designed to address past congressional concerns. Such institutional reforms tend to have a more lasting effect than many statutory reforms, perhaps in part because executive branch officials are directly answerable to the President and perhaps also because they are instituted with more flexibility or sensitivity to the needs of future Presidents. Thus, it makes sense for a new President to follow tradition but also to consider, in time, proposals to improve the process by which executive directives are issued.

Executive Orders Enabled Relief Efforts for Immigrants

Adam B. Cox and Cristina M. Rodríguez

Cristina Rodríguez is the Leighton Homer Surbeck Professor of Law at Yale Law School. Adam Cox is the Robert A. Kindler Professor of Law at New York University.

On November 20, 2014, President Obama announced sweeping executive reforms of immigration law. The centerpiece of his announcement was an initiative designed to provide a measure of security to millions of unauthorized immigrants. Under it, executive branch officials would exercise discretion to defer the deportation of unauthorized immigrants who have lived for years in the United States and have US citizen (or green-card holding) children. Parents who received this "deferred action" also would be eligible to receive work permits. As many as 3.6 million noncitizens may be eligible for relief under the program—a number that jumps to more than five million when the program for parents is combined with an earlier-announced initiative for unauthorized immigrants who arrived in the United States as children. Together, President Obama's efforts could protect nearly fifty percent of today's unauthorized immigrant population.

The President's decision to defer the deportation of millions of immigrants sparked sharp debate among scholars and political figures about his authority to create such a large-scale relief program. The Administration provided an unusually meaty framework for the debate by releasing an opinion, prepared by the Office of Legal Counsel (OLC) in the Department of Justice, concluding that the initiative was well within the Administration's statutory and constitutional authorities. Critics disagreed with OLC's conclusion, decrying President Obama's actions as not just

"The President and Immigration Law Redux," by Adam B. Cox and Cristina M. Rodríguez, *Yale Law Journal*, February 7, 2010. Reprinted by permission.

unwise but unconstitutional—the latest installment in the rise of an imperial presidency. The debate quickly made its way to the federal courts, as nearly two dozen states challenged the relief programs in a lawsuit that, as of this writing, remains pending and has resulted in the temporary injunction of the President's initiatives.

These events have drawn renewed attention to the President's power to shape the substance of immigration law through the exercise of his enforcement power. They have also reignited the longstanding controversy over whether any limits exist on this central source of executive authority. Both of these issues were at the heart of our previous work, The President and Immigration Law. Published in these pages six years ago, that article provided a historical account of the distribution of immigration lawmaking authority between the President and Congress. Our core claim in that piece was that a series of twentieth-century developments—constitutional, historical, and institutional—had, as a functional matter, given the President tremendous power over the immigrant-screening system: power to determine which immigrants would be permitted to remain in the United States, and which would be forced to leave. We labeled this constellation of developments "de facto delegation" and argued that it constituted one of the most important features of modern American immigration law.

Developments since we last wrote, culminating in President Obama's recent announcement, have both confirmed our earlier account and raised important new questions. While our previous work was mostly descriptive and historical, intervening developments have sharpened the legal and theoretical separation of powers questions raised by our argument. Moreover, whereas in 2009 we chiefly addressed the allocation of power between the branches in immigration law, the passage of time has highlighted the importance of power allocations within the Executive Branch for understanding the on-the-ground practice of presidential immigration law. Thus, this Article seeks to move beyond our earlier arguments in two ways—by squarely confronting the legal and normative questions about the President's power over immigration policy, and by carefully unpacking the "unitary" Executive to develop better purchase on these questions and on our earlier descriptive account of the President and immigration law.

This Article makes two central claims about the relationship between enforcement discretion and the separation of powers, both in immigration law and more generally. The first concerns the substantive limits on enforcement discretion: what (if anything) constrains executive branch choices about which immigrants will be protected through the exercise of enforcement discretion? The second concerns the institutionalization of that discretion: what (if anything) constrains executive branch choices about how to institutionalize the exercise of enforcement discretion within the bureaucracy? While we address these questions by focusing on the Obama relief initiatives, the questions themselves implicate broader separation of powers debates and will remain pressing even if opponents of the President's relief initiatives emerge victorious in the pending federal litigation.

With respect to our first argument, we show that efforts to constrain the President's enforcement authority with reference to "congressional enforcement priorities"—an approach taken by both defenders and critics of the President—are doomed to fail. We recognize the appeal of this approach. By tying the exercise of enforcement discretion to inferences about congressional intent drawn directly from immigration statutes, the Administration can claim to be acting as Congress's faithful agent, following the principal's wishes rather than making policy unmoored from the dictates of immigration law's elaborate statutory scheme. On this account, Congress makes the tough value judgments, not the President. He or she simply extracts those underlying value judgments from the statute through sophisticated legal analysis. The approach also provides a seemingly clear limiting principle to prevent the enforcement power from devolving into dispensation of the law—something that supporters of large-scale administrative relief had failed to provide until OLC shifted the tenor of the debate.

The trouble is that this faithful-agent model obscures the role that enforcement discretion plays in our modern system of separated powers. Even outside the immigration context, it would be passing strange to argue that the myriad discretionary decisions made by law enforcement officials should always be motivated and constrained solely or even primarily by the value judgments those officials can trace to a code enacted by Congress. Moreover, this model is especially limited as an account of immigration law. Our historical account of separation of powers in this domain highlights the ubiquity of presidents exercising discretionary immigration authority in ways that cannot be characterized as consistent with clearly identifiable congressional priorities. That history has combined with a series of other developments—most notably the growth of the deportation regime and the size of the unauthorized population—to create the de facto delegation model of immigration policymaking. The tremendous authority wielded by the President under that model to shape our immigrant screening policies renders talk of "congressional priorities" for enforcement inapposite. We do not think it possible to coherently identify a set of congressional priorities for immigration enforcement through a careful, lawyerly exercise of intertextual fidelity to the 300-page immigration code.

Far from fitting into a faithful-agent framework, therefore, our modern system of presidentially driven, ex post immigration screening is better understood as embodying a "two-principals" model of immigration policymaking. One possible response to the emergence of this model would be to decry it as lawless. But that would be a mistake. We see significant value in a model of the enforcement power according to which executive priorities stand alongside congressional ones. As the history of immigration law has demonstrated, this model empowers the Executive to address the unanticipated costs and epistemic limits of ex ante congressional lawmaking, calibrate the policies enacted by Congress to changed circumstances, provoke constructive and innovative policy reforms in both branches, and guard against the perils of legislative stasis. Policymaking through enforcement may not advance these objectives all the time, and it could certainly be abused. But given the reality of de facto delegation and the benefits that flow from the President's current role, it would be a mistake to dismiss policymaking through enforcement as lawless.

While we reject substantive limits derived from congressional priorities, our second claim is that we can still meaningfully address the desirability or legality of particular regimes of enforcement discretion. As we explore in Part III, the better inquiry into the legality of President Obama's relief programs, and the use of the enforcement power more generally, asks whether the Executive should be constitutionally prohibited from institutionalizing enforcement discretion in particular ways. The most important aspects of the President's immigration initiatives have nothing to do with the substantive criteria for relief; the program's focus on children, families, long-term residence, and clean criminal records strongly resembles the approach contained in many earlier, much less controversial guidance documents intended to channel prosecutorial discretion. Instead, the more important innovation was to make the exercise of discretion more rule-like, centralized, and transparent. These features have been the focus of prominent critics, who have argued that the President has wielded prosecutorial discretion in an impermissibly "categorical" way, rather than in a valid "individualized" fashion, or that he has extended substantive "legal benefits" to unauthorized immigrants, rather than mere forbearance.

The institutional choices embodied in the President's initiatives thus raise issues far beyond immigration law: they concern broader debates about centralization, transparency, and bureaucratic justice. How one evaluates the choices embodied in the President's plans, therefore, cannot be divorced entirely from one's views on some classic debates about the theoretical and legal underpinnings of the American administrative state. In that sense, the President's critics are correct that much more is at stake than the justice of deferring the removal of long-term residents of the United States.

At the same time, critics err in thinking that those debates can be resolved in this instance without a historically grounded understanding of the immigration separation of powers. The institutional account of immigration law that we have jointly developed over the course of the last several years ultimately helps explain exactly why the President's immigration initiatives are both lawful and desirable. They promote important rule-of-law values, such as transparency and accountability, as well as the age-old aim of treating like cases alike. And they do so without threatening to undermine another rule-of-law value—legal compliance— that some have claimed will be compromised by the President's initiatives. Conjuring out of Article II ether a constitutional prohibition on the way the President has institutionalized discretion in his recent immigration initiatives would significantly undermine these values, and for essentially no benefit. Moreover, it would entrench the authority of low-level bureaucrats against alternative judgments about how best to arrange power within the bureaucracy—even judgments by the very Congress that created the bureaucracy.

Our complementary arguments—against the congressional priorities approach and in favor of a focus on discretion's institutionalization—ultimately show how the leading critiques of the President's relief initiatives go wrong. Yet our two central claims are important not only (or even primarily) because they help us properly evaluate the legality of the most important presidential immigration initiative in several decades. They also address a set of shortcomings in modern separation of powers and administrative law theory. Principal-agent models borrowed from contract theory and positive political theory have been invaluable tools for analyzing the administrative state. But those models also have serious limitations. In this Article, we illuminate one crucial area of executive power where standard principal-agent models obscure much more than they illuminate. We also show that the project of fleshing out separation of powers theory, descriptively and normatively, must occur with much more institutional and domain-specific context than is typical in contemporary constitutional scholarship. Far from an argument for immigration exceptionalism, our analysis highlights how immigration is just like multiple other domains of regulation, in that each evolves according to particular legal, practical, and political dynamics. Though we may be able to identify abstract goals that a system of separated powers should serve, how power has been and ought to be allocated among the branches to serve those goals will differ across time and setting.

This emphasis on context does not mean that the search for generalizable limiting principles or theories in separation of powers contexts is doomed. In fact, the arguments we make in Parts II and III together provide a framework, which we develop in Part IV, for thinking about limiting principles that can serve separation of powers values while accounting for institutional and historical context. Moreover, our defenses of presidential immigration law in general, and President Obama's immigration initiatives in particular, do not amount to a conclusion that current congressional-executive dynamics are optimal. We conclude in Part IV, therefore, by taking seriously the second-best nature of immigration law's current structure. We consider reforms—both modest and radical—that would promote and discipline the role that the President currently plays in American immigration law.

I. A Brief History of Presidential Immigration Law

Before we can evaluate the immigration enforcement initiatives announced by President Obama and understand the scope of the contemporary enforcement power, some history is in order. This Part situates the initiatives within a century-long story of administrative innovation that produced modern American immigration law. Only with this context can we make sense of the motivations for, and the legality of, the President's deportation relief programs.

We show that the Obama relief initiatives represent only the most recent examples of the executive policymaking that has been part and parcel of immigration history. The President has always been an immigration policymaker alongside and sometimes in competition with Congress. President Obama's recent actions simply reinforce the ways in which the content and scope of the President's regulatory authority have evolved in response to the actions of Congress, as well as underlying historical and social factors. That evolution has been complex, involving a combination of partisan politics, economic and demographic forces, social movement pressures, and institutional demands. This specificity of context, however, does not turn our account into a tyranny of particularism. The trajectory we trace provides important, generalizable lessons that, as we will show in Parts II and III, have direct implications for how we judge the legality and desirability of the President's relief initiatives and the use of the enforcement power more generally.

These lessons ultimately differ considerably from the ones that some supporters of the President's initiatives have drawn from pieces of the history we recount below. Some commentators have argued that the initiatives are lawful because they sufficiently resemble actions by previous administrations—in particular, the use of administrative relief by Presidents Reagan and Bush during the implementation of a legalization program enacted by Congress in 1986. We neither treat this history as quasi-legal precedent, nor rely on debatable notions of congressional acquiescence to executive branch practice to make claims about constitutional settlements between the branches. Instead, we use this history to provide a thorough account of the structure of modern immigration law, identify the imperatives and temptations that attend the use of the enforcement power in light of that structure, and explain the motivations for present-day uses of that power. Our history underscores what critics fail to understand about the nature of enforcement today, and in that sense it provides the context for a reality-based articulation of the scope of the enforcement power.

In this Part, we begin by summarizing our 2009 account of how the President historically has used the powers expressly delegated to him to advance his own policy agenda, resulting in what we term executive unilateralism. We then turn to the central source of power at issue in this Article—enforcement discretion. We demonstrate how the underenforcement of certain parts of the immigration code, as in many domains, has transformed the law enacted by Congress into regulation that reflects executive branch priorities. We then elaborate on the concept of de facto delegation introduced in our earlier work and explain its relevance to current controversies. In keeping with our focus on the internal organization of the Executive Branch, we close by documenting the trend in recent decades toward the Executive's centralization of its enforcement discretion. Taken together, these perspectives on executive power help make the descriptive case for the two-principals model defended in Part II and provide the institutional detail required to understand what precisely is at stake with the Obama relief initiatives.

[...]

The Legislative Process Is Too Slow and Complicated

Union of Concerned Scientists

The Union of Concerned Scientists is a nonprofit science advocacy organization based in the United States. Its membership includes private citizens and professional scientists.

As you will learn below, there are any number of places that a bill can get lost on the way to becoming a law, and most do just that. Thousands of bills are introduced into Congress each session, and only several hundred get signed into law. Fewer still establish substantive policy, since most bills passed by Congress deal with non-controversial issues such as the naming of a post office. Those bills that make or change important policies only pass as a result of deep commitment by the public or other interested parties. With each positive step forward—such as a new piece of legislation—the voices of the status quo continue to use the politics of fear, attempting to delay action and promote their own short-term interests. That's why UCS, our coalition partners, and our activists have to be there at every step of the process, making sure that Congress passes strong, science-based legislation to make our world cleaner and safer, strengthen the economy, and enhance national security.

Bill Introduction

Although the concept for a piece of legislation can come from anyone, only a member of Congress can introduce a bill. In the House of Representatives, the lawmaker places the bill in the *hopper*—a box located on the House Clerk's desk—and in the Senate, the lawmaker introduces the bill on the Senate floor with recognition from the presiding officer. Members may demonstrate

"The U.S. Legislative Process," Union of Concerned Scientists. Reprinted by permission.

formal support for a colleague's proposal by becoming *co-sponsors* of the bill.

After the bill is assigned a number, it is referred to the relevant committee for their careful review. The entire bill or pieces of it may also be referred to other appropriate committees or to a subcommittee for more specialized review.

In Subcommittee

If a bill is sent to a subcommittee, the members of the subcommittee may hold hearings to gather the testimony of experts, supporters, and opponents of the bill. *Amendments*, or changes to the bill proposed by members of Congress, are debated and then voted on for acceptance or rejection during a *mark up* session. The subcommittee then votes on whether to report the bill and its amendments back to the full committee. A subcommittee may *table* a bill if it decides to stop action on it.

In Committee

Similar to a subcommittee, when a bill is in committee, the members of the committee may hold hearings to gather the testimony of experts, supporters, and opponents of the bill. *Amendments,* or changes to the bill proposed by members of Congress, are debated and voted on for acceptance or rejection during a *mark up* session. If there are substantial amendments to the bill, the committee may introduce a clean version with a new bill number. Following mark up, the committee votes on whether to report the bill and its amendments out of committee and send it to the House or Senate floor. Like a subcommittee, a full committee may *table* a bill if it decides to stop action on it.

Floor Action

After passing out of full committee, the bill is placed on the calendar for House or Senate "floor action." In the House, the Rules Committee will determine the rules that govern floor action, such as the length of debate or whether amendments can be offered.

During floor action, members debate the bill and offer amendments (if allowed). In the House, amendments must be germane to the subject of the bill, but not in the Senate. As such, senators may introduce *riders*, or irrelevant amendments. And while the length of debate is usually limited by the Rules Committee in the House, there is no limit in the Senate, thus enabling senators to *filibuster*, or delay/prevent a vote with extended debate. Three-fifths of the senate or 60 votes are needed to invoke *cloture*, or end debate. Since filibusters are common for any controversial bill in the Senate, such bills generally require 60 votes to end debate and allow an up or down vote. When a bill is put to an up or down vote in either chamber, a quorum of members must be in attendance on the floor and a majority (218 votes in the House and 51 votes in the Senate) of "aye" votes are needed for passage. The bill is considered *engrossed* when it has been passed out of the chamber and certified by the Clerk. It is then referred to the other chamber unless a similar bill is already undergoing the legislative process in that chamber. Legislation must pass out of both chambers in order to continue toward becoming law.

Conference Committee

Especially with major legislation, there are likely to be differences between the two bills passed out of the House and Senate. Conferees are designated from both chambers to negotiate and find consensus on conflicting provisions and the final conference report is sent back to the House and Senate for approval. Once the bill has been approved by both chambers, it is sent to the president, where the bill is considered *enrolled.*

President

The president has several options to take with the enrolled bill:

- The president does not take action and the bill automatically becomes law after 10 days when Congress is in session.
- The president does not take action and the bill dies because Congress is not in session. This is referred to as a *pocket veto.*

- The president vetoes the bill and sends it back to the chamber where it originated from with a report of the reasons for the veto.
- The president signs the bill and it becomes law.

Bill Becomes Law

There are three ways a bill can become law:

- The president does not take action and it automatically becomes law after 10 days when Congress is in session.
- The president signs the bill.
- Congress overrides the presidential veto and the bill becomes law. A two-thirds majority vote is needed in both chambers to override the veto.

Congress.gov is a Library of Congress website where you can track the status of legislation and find other information, such as the text of the bill and amendments, co-sponsor lists, and vote results.

Are Executive Orders Vital in Times of National Emergency?

What Is the Role of the President?

James E. Hanley

James E. Hanley is an associate professor of political science at Adrian College and a fellow of the Institute for Social Policy and Understanding.

The Basics of the Presidency

Role: Chief Executive (Head of the Executive Branch).

Term of Office: 4 years: Originally no limit on number of terms, but now a constitutional limit of 2 terms + a maximum of 2 years of a predecessor's term (22nd Amendment), for a maximum of 10 years.

Qualifications: Minimum age of 35 years; natural born citizen of the United States; 14 years a resident within the United States.

Presidential Power

Presidents claim powers from three different sources: 1) the Constitution, 2) Congressional delegation, and 3) the inherent powers of the executive.

- *Constitutional Powers*
  The Constitution specifically grants the President a small number of powers. These constitutional powers are: 1) being the Commander-in-Chief of the armed forces, 2) the power to make treaties with other countries, 3) the power to appoint and receive ambassadors from other countries, 4) the power to appoint other officers in the executive branch (with Senate approval), and 5) the power to federal judges, including Supreme Court justices (all subject to Senate approval).

"The Role and Functions of the Presidency," by James E. Hanley, College American Government, 2014. Reprinted by permission.

- *Delegated Powers*

  Although Congress theoretically cannot delegate actual legislative authority to the Executive branch, it has delegated substantial power to presidents to shape public policy. An important example is the Budget and Accounting Act of 1921, a statute requiring the President to annually submit a proposed US budget for Congress to consider. Congress also frequently writes vague laws and gives the executive branch considerable discretion in writing rules to implement the law, both because they lack the technical expertise and because it is easy to gain support for vague laws that sound like they are for a good cause while letting the executive branch be the target of criticism for any unpopular details and costs of implementing the law.

- *Inherent Powers*

  Most controversial, presidents claim that there are "inherent powers"—powers that naturally and inevitably attach to the very fact of being the chief executive. Because these powers are just inferred from the nature of executive authority, there is no explicit or official list of such powers, just powers that Presidents have claimed, and that Congress and the Courts have accepted. The power to make executive agreements and executive orders (see below) are among these inherent powers. Also among these powers is the claim of *executive privilege*, the authority of the President to determine what information from the Executive Branch can be released to Congress. Executive privilege serves two purposes. First, it ensures that military and diplomatic secrets can be kept within the Executive branch and not made public. Second, it enables presidents to get candid advice from their advisors, who do not have to guard their words for fear they will be made public. As part of executive privilege, when Congress invites Executive branch officials to testify, they can only do so if the President approves.

Roles of the Presidency

> The executive power shall be vested in a President of the United States of America...he shall take care that the laws be faithfully executed (US Constitution, Article II)

The President is the chief executive of the United States, responsible primarily for 1) ensuring that the laws passed by Congress are put into force effectively and 2) being the United States' representative to the rest of the world. Of course the President cannot single-handedly execute all the laws of the United States or make all decisions concerning US relations with other countries, so the executive branch also contains a large number of federal agencies to support these presidential responsibilities.

Head of Government and Head of State

As *head of government* the President is involved in the daily running of the government and making policy. In a parliamentary system this is the role of the Prime Minister. As head of government presidents promotes policies they favor, pressuring Congress to pass legislation to their liking and trying to block legislation they dislike. The President also heads up the executive branch agencies as they make decisions about the carrying out of the country's laws. As we noted in the chapters on Congress, they often write laws vaguely, allowing the executive agencies to write rules—called *federal regulations*—to fill in the details. For example, in filling in the details of the Clean Air Act, the Environmental Protection Agency has created rules governing plywood manufacturers that emit 10 tons or more each year of any designated hazardous air pollutant, or 25 tons of a combination of hazardous air pollutants. A president who supports stronger environmental protections might ask the EPA to revise the rule to cover more plywood manufacturers, perhaps those producing at least 15 tons of hazardous pollutants per year, while a president who thinks environmental regulations are already too strict might ask the EPA to consider changing the rule to increase the allowable amounts of hazardous air pollutants emitted.

As head of government, presidents operate in a policy-making role, which makes them a divisive force in American politics simply because the public has disagreements about policy. When Barack Obama announced that the government would not deport young illegal immigrants whose parents brought them to the US as children, many Americans supported his choice of how to enforce immigration law, and many opposed it. When Donald Trump reversed that policy and began deporting those young immigrants, some supported the new policy but many didn't. Presidents cannot avoid taking sides in such debates because they have to choose how they will enforce laws. As *head of state* the President represents the whole country, and tries to *unite*, rather than divide, the public. In a constitutional monarchy, the king or queen fulfills the role of head of state. In a constitutional monarchy, a king or queen fulfills the role of head of state, such as Queen Elizabeth, who stands as a symbol of the U.K. but does not engage in policymaking. In the US, the President plays the head of state role when he steps outside of everyday politics, to act in a way that represents the US as a whole. It also includes a variety of symbolic actions presidents take, from personally reviewing disaster-stricken areas to meeting with championship sports teams. For example, after the 9/11 terrorist attacks George W. Bush visited the site of the collapsed World Trade Center. There was no policy need for the President to go there, and he did not go as a Republican or as a conservative, but as the American president.

Americans expect their presidents to take such symbolic actions. When Hurricane Katrina flooded New Orleans, Bush was criticized for simply observing the devastation from the air rather than touring it on the ground. Bush himself has said this was a "big mistake," and that the photos of him looking out the window made him look "detached and uncaring."[1] The criticisms were a bit silly. Not only is an aerial view a good way to get perspective on a wide-ranging disaster, but Bush could make decisions from his plane or from the White House as easily as he could with his feet in the water. But Presidents are constrained not by what makes sense; they are constrained by what the public demands of them. And if Bush had actually landed in New Orleans he could have had pictures taken of him meeting victims and consoling them, or praising relief workers. For presidents, it is not enough to care; the public demands a *display* of care.

These dual roles of head of government and head of state, of divisive policymaker and uniting symbol of America, create one of any President's biggest challenges. The Queen of Great Britain can focus on being a symbol for the whole country because she isn't expected to get involved in politics, and the British Prime Minister can focus on passing their party's favored policies against other parties' opposition. But US presidents are expected to be both a symbol of the country and a partisan political warrior, and few can balance those conflicting roles well.

[…]

Chief Legislator

> He shall from time to time give to the Congress information of the state of the union, and recommend to their consideration such measures as he shall judge necessary and expedient; (Article II, §3, US Constitution).

Presidential scholar Richard Neustadt famously observed that the Constitution does not really create a system of separation of powers but one of separated institutions *sharing* powers.[6] Although the President is not part of the legislative branch, the Constitution gives clear authorization to get involved in the legislative process, and because of the President's significant influence the role of chief legislator falls within the President's role as head of government. Because every president knows their legacy depends in part on how effective they are at legislation, and because they ran for the presidency with specific policy goals and made promises to the American public, influencing legislation is among a president's most important concerns.

Although the Constitution is vague about how often the President should give Congress information about the state of the union, and in what manner the information should be given, this duty has evolved into the annual State of the Union address—watched not only by Americans, but by people around the world—in which the President declares a set of policy goals for the coming year. Constitutionally, presidents could just send occasional notes to Congress giving them factual information, such as the unemployment rate and international threats to interests, without appearing before the public or making specific policy proposals, but the televised State of the Union Address, with lots of pomp and ceremony, is an important agenda-setting opportunity, and no modern president would pass up the opportunity.

The President is constitutionally authorized to propose legislation, submitting bills to Congress that "recommend to their consideration such measures as he shall judge necessary and expedient." These bills are likely to be taken seriously by members of the President's party, but may face stiff opposition from the opposition party. Presidents can also get actively involved in the legislative process by negotiating with Congress. Sometimes they do this indirectly, directing their advisers to pressure and negotiate with Congressmembers, and when the stakes are high they will often engage legislators directly. Presidents may talk to them by phone or may invited them to meet in the Oval Office in order to pressure them for support of his proposed policies.

The President's most powerful legislative tool is the veto power. If a president vetoes a bill passed by Congress, it takes a two-thirds vote in each house of Congress to override and make the bill law. Although the veto comes at the end of the process, its effects reach forward to the start of the process, as congressional leaders must consider whether the President will find a bill acceptable or not, and if not, whether they have enough votes to override his veto. If not, they have to decide whether to give up on the bill, try to change it enough to get presidential support, or force a veto in the hopes that they will gain public approval for their position. Very few presidential vetoes are overridden, both because congressional leaders will reshape legislation in cases where it is possible to get presidential approval and because presidents pay attention to how much support a bill has and rarely employ the veto when they know there are enough votes in Congress to override it.

A controversial way presidents act as legislators is through signing statements. When signing a bill into law, presidents normally make some commentary about the law, and what they see as its meaning and significance. In recent presidencies, most notably in the presidency of George W. Bush, the signing statement became a substitute for veto battles. Bush frequently signed bills into law while asserting that certain parts trespassed on executive authority, and therefore were unconstitutional and would not be enforced. While presidents have always had a considerable amount of leeway in the implementation and enforcement of laws, this blunt statement that the President had authority to pick and choose which parts of the law he would enforce was a step beyond the traditional authority of the executive, and remains controversial.

Presidents also play a legislative role at the direct order of Congress, through the delegated authority and requirement to propose an annual budget for the United States. Congress is constitutionally responsible for determining the federal government's spending, as Article I, §9 of the Constitution requires that "No money shall be drawn from the treasury, but in consequence of appropriations made by law." But Congress often finds it hard to develop a budget on its own, and in 1921 passed the Budget and Accounting Act, requiring the president to submit a budget proposal. The fate of presidents' budget proposals depends on the level of support they have in Congress. It helps to have their own party in the majority in both houses, although that is no guarantee they'll get everything they want. Each Congressmember is concerned about how the budget affects his or her own constituents. But it is harder for presidents to get their way when the opposing party controls one or both houses.

Despite the challenges, the budget proposal is an important agenda-setting opportunity for presidents. If you want to know any organization's real goals, you have to look not at what it says its goals are, but where it spends its money. So by making decisions about how much money to spend on what policies, budgeting is the most fundamentally important set of policy decisions the government makes. For example a law requiring that a wall be built on the Mexican-American border is only effective if enough money is appropriated to build it, and a president can press for more funding or less, depending on whether a border wall is a priority to them. By setting the agenda on those decisions, and wielding the veto at the back end of the budgeting process, a canny President can exert significant influence in shaping public policy.

A final way presidents are de facto legislators is through executive orders. Executive orders do not need approval of Congress because they refer only to the operations of the executive branch of government, and are part of a president's responsibility to manage the executive branch. But they do have important policy effects. George W. Bush authorized "enhanced interrogation techniques," widely viewed as torture, to be used against terrorism suspects, and Barack Obama issued an executive order repealing the Bush order.[7] Another Obama executive order enforced sanctions on North Korea by prohibiting the importation of any goods from the country.[8] And on a more mundane level a Clinton executive order streamlined the executive branch's process for procuring office supplies.

Summary

The President is the country's chief executive, responsible for ensuring the laws are faithfully executed, managing the executive branch of the government, promoting politics through legislation and rule-making, and representing the US in international relations. They are also asked to be both head of government and head of state, roles that conflict with each other in how they relate to the American public. In performing their duties presidents draw on their constitutional powers, powers delegated by Congress, and their own claims of inherent executive powers, and they are aided by the institutional presidency, particularly the Executive

Office of the President. Compared to Congress Presidents have a unique ability to command the attention of the American public, but their public approvals inevitably decline over time, eroding their ability to be an effective policy leader as their time in office draws to a close.

Notes

1. Brower, Kate Anderson, and Catherine Dodge. 2010. "Bush Says New Orleans Flyover After Katrina a "Huge Mistake." Bloomberg.com. Nov. 5. http://www.bloomberg.com/news/2010-11-05/bush-calls-new-orleansflyover-in-wake-of-hurricane-katrina-huge-mistake-.html.

2. Rossiter, Clinton. 1956/1960. *The American President*, 2nd ed. New York: Mentor Books. p.28.

3. United States Senate. "Pending." http://www.state.gov/s/l/treaty/pending/.

4 .United States Senate. "Treaties."

http://www.senate.gov/artandhistory/history/common/briefing/Treaties.htm

5. ibid.

6. Neustadt, Richard. 1960. *Presidential Power*. New York: Signet books. P42

7. Executive Order 13491—Ensuring Lawful Interrogations.

8. Executive Order 13570—Prohibiting Certain Transactions with Respect to North Korea.

9. Kernell, Samual H. 2006. *Going Public: New Strategies of Presidential Leadership*. Washington, D.C.: CQ Press.

Treating the Opioid Crisis as a National Emergency Could Allow Something to Be Done About It

Alison Kodjak

Alison Kodjak is a health policy correspondent on National Public Radio's Science Desk.

Opioid abuse is a crisis, but is it an emergency?

That's the question gripping Washington after President Trump's Commission on Combating Drug Addiction and the Opioid Crisis recommended that the president declare the epidemic a national emergency.

On Tuesday, before getting a briefing on the commission report, Trump called it "a tremendous problem."

"We're going to get it taken care of," he said.

Later that day, Health and Human Services Secretary Tom Price backed off from the need for an emergency declaration.

"We believe that, at this point, that the resources that we need, or the focus that we need to bring to bear to the opioid crisis can be addressed without the declaration of an emergency," he said, adding that the option was still on the table.

On Thursday, the president availed himself of that option.

"The opioid crisis is an emergency, and I'm saying officially right now: It is an emergency," Trump said at an impromptu press briefing at his golf club in Bedminster, N.J.

The White House followed up with a press release saying the president "has instructed his Administration to use all appropriate emergency and other authorities to respond to the crisis caused by the opioid epidemic."

So while the president has announced an emergency, he and his administration haven't formally declared one—a process that comes with specific legal authority and brings specific sets of powers and access to money.

You can see a series of formal public health emergency declarations here.

If the president does move ahead and declare the opioid crisis an emergency, here's what could happen.

FEMA Money Could Be Available to States

The president could use authority under the Stafford Act to declare an emergency. That would open up resources that are usually reserved for natural disasters like hurricanes or floods, including FEMA's disaster relief fund, which had about $1.5 billion available as of July.

Public Health Workers Could Be Redeployed

The president could ask HHS Secretary Price to declare an emergency under the Public Health Service Act. Unlike FEMA, HHS doesn't have a standing emergency fund (although during last year's Zika virus scare, many people urged that one be established), but money could be freed up. Right now, public health workers and researchers are working on projects defined by grants from HHS. If Price were to declare an emergency, those workers could be redeployed temporarily, from working on AIDS outreach for example, to work on substance abuse issues.

Access to Medication-Assisted Treatment Could Get a Boost

In a public health emergency, the HHS secretary could make it easier to get medications to counter addiction. For example, Price could allow "standing orders" for the drug naloxone, used to reverse overdoses, which would allow certain populations to get the medication without a prescription. He could also waive the restrictions on doctors who want to administer methadone or buprenorphine to patients with opioid addictions. Those medications currently require a prescribing doctor to have special certification, and there are limits to the number of people doctors can treat.

Medicaid Could Pay for More Treatment

A public health emergency would also allow HHS to waive certain regulations. One major target could be a rule that restricts where Medicaid patients can get inpatient drug treatment. If HHS waived that rule, then Medicaid beneficiaries might find it easier to get treatment.

Congress Could Appropriate Money

Congress doesn't need an emergency declaration to appropriate money for more drug treatment and intervention. But if the Trump administration were to issue such an order, it would put a lot of pressure on Congress to back it up with money. Last year, lawmakers passed a law to address addiction issues but refused to include $1.1 billion that President Barack Obama requested to expand treatment programs.

States Could Request Aid

Six states have already declared opioid emergencies. A federal emergency could open up paths for those states to request federal grants for specific purposes. Maryland, for example, has a tool that tracks overdoses in real time so emergency responders can identify where particularly potent synthetic opioids may be on the streets. Federal money could potentially allow other states to follow suit.

The Great Depression: Lessons on Effective Executive Orders

Jeanne Mirer and Marjorie Cohn

Jeanne Mirer is a lawyer who practices civil rights and employment law. Marjorie Cohn is a professor emerita at Thomas Jefferson School of Law, where she taught for twenty-five years.

On May 6, 1935, with the country in the midst of the Great Depression, and with indirect efforts to create jobs having not moved the needle of unemployment rates, President Franklin D. Roosevelt signed Executive Order 7034 and appropriated $4.8 billion for the Works Progress Administration (WPA). The WPA put millions of Americans to work constructing buildings, painting murals to decorate them, and performing plays for audiences that had never before seen a dramatic production. In the process, many were saved from poverty and starvation and the economy began to revive.

Although Congress, as part of the New Deal, had appropriated money specifically for relief, FDR decided to use the money for a direct jobs program by issuing a Presidential executive order. This Executive Order described the agencies to be involved in the program, its structure and procedure for application and allocation of jobs.

The WPA was quickly implemented. By March 1936, 3.4 million people were employed and an average of 2.3 million people worked monthly until the program ended in June 1943. During its existence the WPA employed more than 8,500,000 different persons on 1,410,000 individual projects, and spent about $11 billion. The average yearly salary was $1,100, a living wage at the time. During its 8-year history, the WPA built 651,087 miles of highways, roads,

"Lessons of the Great Depression of the 1930s: Create Jobs by Executive Order," by Jeanne Mirer and Marjorie Cohn, GlobalResearch.ca, November 8, 2010. Reprinted by permission.

and streets. It constructed, repaired, or improved 124,031 bridges, 125,110 public buildings, 8,192 parks, and 853 airport landing fields.

Today our infrastructure is crumbling, and loss of revenue is forcing many cities and states to cut basic services. About 15 million people have become unemployed since the crisis hit in late 2008; a million and a half of them are construction workers. The need for a direct jobs program is either as great, or even greater than during the Depression.

But, in light of the election results, is such a program possible? Can the President directly create jobs by executive order? The answer is a resounding yes. Remember when the Emergency Economic Stabilization Act of 2008, which created the $700 billion Troubled Assets Relief Program (TARP) was passed, one of the purposes was to preserve homeownership, and promote jobs and economic growth.

Much of the TARP money has been repaid and the administration refers to the profit on the payments. If one assumes an average cost of one job is $50,000, 6 million jobs could be immediately created for $300 billion. 12 million jobs could be created for $600 billion. Because this is already appropriated money, Congressional Republicans could not block it.

This direct job creation would be bold. It would also be highly stimulative. It would not add to the deficit because it is already appropriated money. Furthermore, one third of it would come back immediately in taxes, and more importantly, the growth in demand from this number of added jobs would expand private sector job growth and grow the overall economy.

This bold program would contrast markedly with prior stimulus bills, which were indirect and whose effects have been too slow to manifest themselves. The posture of the Republicans during the last two years has been to prevent the President and Congress from taking bold steps to intervene in the economy to directly create jobs. Then they used the Administration's failure to take bold steps to create jobs to say the "stimulus did not work." They turned the very TARP bailouts they supported into a rallying cry against government intervention in the economy to help people and they characterized as "socialism" any government initiatives such as health care. They decried deficits and opposed any sane tax policies to get the deficit going in the other direction.

By keeping progress in job creation slow and blaming the administration for lack of jobs, the high expectations for the Obama administration became deflated. The loss of jobs exacerbated the mortgage crisis, and banks have been encouraged to foreclose rather than restructure mortgages despite the opposite being explicitly called for the Emergency Stabilization Act.

The people who voted for Obama in 2008 voted for the promised hope and change. Many developed buyer's remorse when what they got a set of policies which protected Wall Street at the expense of Main Street, big business at the expense of workers, and made unnecessary compromises with the right. The so called "enthusiasm gap" created by Republican obstruction and Administration timidity, produced such a deflation in people's morale that it acted as an effective form of voter suppression. The election results can be explained in this fashion.

Some have said that it makes no sense that the voters would go in a more rightward direction because the Obama administration was not "left" enough. But the fact is the Obama administration failed to deliver change and also failed to make the case for progressive policies. The election of Democratic incumbents meant only more of the same. And only 9 million of the 23 million young people who voted in 2008, came out in 2010. This undervote made the difference.

Abraham Lincoln once said: "You can fool some of the people all of the time, and all of the people some of the time but you cannot fool all of the people all of the time." What happened in this election was the right wing was able to fool enough of the people enough of the time to make independents join with rabid right wingers, while at the same time suppressing the progressive electorate.

This country has a lot to do to get its economic house in order. It is heavily dependent on the financial services industry which only promotes speculation and unregulated bubbles. It is largely controlled by the defense industries which have promoted two and possibly more wars. It is beholden to the extractive energy industries, whose owners are funding the "tea party," thus putting environmental amelioration on indefinite hold. And it is more and more influenced by the prison industrial complex which promotes hostility to immigrants, and takes resources from education and other vital areas. For the last 30 years it has relied on anti-union and anti-worker policies, which has forced the hemorrhaging of high paid manufacturing jobs to low cost countries and driven down wages for US workers which can no longer be papered over with unsustainable debt.

The President cannot solve all these problems overnight, but with a stroke of a pen he can use already appropriated money to create millions of good green jobs, and move down the road to recovery much faster. Any opposition to this from the Republicans will expose their hostility to anyone but the richest members of society, and give the progressive movement ammunition to take the offensive.

Regulatory Reforms Made by Executive Order Do Not Last

Environmental Law Institute

The Environmental Law Institute is an internationally recognized, nonpartisan research and education center working to strengthen environmental protection by improving law and governance worldwide.

All presidential administrations employ a wide variety of executive orders and other executive actions, which serve important organizational, symbolic, and policy purposes. However, this presidential power is limited: it largely consists of directives to the executive branch, it must be in accordance with the law, and its exercise is readily subject to modification or reversal by a successor president. The Obama White House's presidential actions on environment and climate change likely will be subject to modification.

Reversing or Revising Executive Orders and Actions

Actor: President

Process

Presidents issue a vast number of executive orders, proclamations, memoranda, and other instruments ranging widely in their purpose and effect, from internal management directives to sweeping changes in federal policy to exercises of military command. In the environmental field, these actions might be implemented in several ways: by the White House itself, through the Council on Environmental Quality (CEQ) or EPA, or via interagency coordination.

Except in the unusual case where Congress has authorized the President to make decisions having legal effect, executive

"Regulatory Reform in the Trump Era," Environmental Law Institute, March 2017. Reprinted by permission.

orders are not lawmaking in the ordinary sense. Rather, they are directives to be followed within the executive branch, by virtue of the president's inherent power to appoint or remove agency heads and other officials. But to bind government agencies and withstand judicial review, executive orders must be consistent with and operate within the limits of applicable law, whether found in the Constitution or statute. An executive order can be revoked or modified by the president who issued it or a successor president; by an act of Congress, if the president was acting on authority granted by Congress; or by a court ruling that the order was illegal or unconstitutional.

Discussion

Especially in times of political gridlock, the idea of making sweeping changes "with the stroke of a pen" can be appealing, and presidents do advance some substantive policy goals through their orders affecting agencies' structure, statutory interpretations, enforcement priorities, or contracting and procurement. But it is equally easy for a successor administration to alter or reverse these policies, and such changes routinely occur with a change of parties.

A new administration typically also takes executive action to temporarily freeze still-pending agency rules, but longer or indefinite delays may be subject to challenge in court.[1] Executive orders cannot unilaterally revoke an agency rule that is already on the books, but they may direct the agency to begin the process of reviewing the rule and revising or withdrawing it through a subsequent rulemaking.

Opportunities for Public Engagement

There is minimal opportunity for interested parties to engage in the development of presidential actions, and often no recourse afterwards in the courts. The only direct channel for affecting executive action is through discussions with White House staff. Congressional engagement is another possibility, but Congress rarely intervenes, and any resulting legislation would be subject to a presidential veto. Courts may be called upon to review the legality of executive orders; but the mere revocation of existing orders is unlikely to provide a legal basis for a lawsuit, nor is it clear who would have standing to sue.

Action Areas to Watch

Executive Order No. 13547, "Stewardship of the Ocean, Our Coasts, and the Great Lakes" (2010); Executive Order No. 13653, "Preparing the United States for the Impacts of Climate Change" (2013); Executive Order No. 13693, "Planning for Federal Sustainability in the Next Decade" (2015); Presidential Memorandum on Power Sector Carbon Pollution Standards (2013); President's Climate Action Plan (2013); CEQ Guidance on Consideration of Greenhouse Gas Emissions and the Effects of Climate Change in NEPA Reviews (2016); Interagency Working Group on Social Cost of Carbon.

Relevant Trump Administration Executive Actions

Presidential Memorandum on "Regulatory Freeze Pending Review" (Jan. 20, 2017); Executive Order Expediting Environmental Reviews and Approvals for High Priority Infrastructure Projects (Jan. 24); Presidential Memoranda Regarding Construction of the Keystone and Dakota Access Pipelines (Jan. 24); Executive Order Reducing Regulation and Controlling Regulatory Costs (Jan. 30); Executive Order on Enforcing the Regulatory Reform Agenda (Feb. 24); Executive Order on Reviewing the "Waters of the United States" Rule (Feb. 28).

Undoing Presidential Actions Protecting Public Lands and Resources

Actors: President, Congress

National Monuments

Sixteen presidents, including Presidents Barack Obama and George W. Bush, have used their authority under the Antiquities Act of 1906 to create national monuments by "public proclamation." 54 U.S.C. § 320301. These proclamations set aside federal lands and waters that contain "historic landmarks, historic and prehistoric structures, and other objects of historic or scientific interest," and protect these resources from incompatible activities such as mining, leasing, logging, grazing, collecting, commercial fishing, and other uses. Under the Act, these monument reservations are to be the "smallest area compatible with the proper care and management of the objects to be protected," which courts nonetheless have recognized can include huge acreages.

Leasing Withdrawals

In addition, Section 12(a) of the Outer Continental Shelf Lands Act (OCSLA), 43 U.S.C. § 1341(a), grants the president authority "from time to time, to withdraw from disposition any of the unleased lands" of the outer continental shelf. This authority has been used by six presidents to establish and maintain temporary oil and gas leasing moratoria as well as to create permanent protected areas. President Obama recently withdrew certain areas of the OCS, including large portions of the US Arctic and the underwater canyon complexes off the Atlantic Coast, from leasing for exploration, development or production "for a time period without specific expiration." Section 12(a) does not provide explicit criteria for the exercise of this withdrawal power.

Notes
1. E.g., *Sierra Club v. Jackson*, 833 F. Supp.2d 11, 26-28 (D.D.C. 2012).

The Way Presidents Use Executive Orders Abuses Their Original Intentions

Brandon Schmuck

Brandon Schmuck has a degree in electrical and computer engineering from Carnegie Mellon University. He works in the tech industry.

The countless headlines last week have left a number of Americans questioning the lack of limits on authority that has been granted to presidents through executive orders. This fear is justifiable, as the idea of any individual having the power to make such orders is both frightening and a risk to the welfare of this nation. However, this is nothing new and is something that should have been considered long before the election of President Trump.

With Trump's immigration order, we saw just how damaging this kind of policy can be to the nation if left unchecked. Is this newfound concern a result of recent times, or something that has been left unchecked throughout the history of our nation?

Executive orders date to the beginning of this nation and originate from Article II of the Constitution, through which the president is granted "executive power." It directs presidents to "take care that the laws be faithfully executed." This does not give the president the authority to create new laws or allocate new funding from the treasury. It simply allows them to use laws and funding that already exist to carry out actions.

As controversial as they may be, most executive orders simply enforce ignored laws that have existed for years. Trump's wall order did not allocate new funding to the building of a wall. It simply directed the Department of Homeland Security to use existing funding to expand the physical barriers at the border. Something as significant as a border fence that costs billions

"Presidents' Use of Executive Orders Abuses Original Intentions," by Brandon Schmuck, *Tartan*, February 5, 2017. Reprinted by permission.

must go through Congress for legitimacy. The Secure Fence Act of 2006, which called for 700 miles of physical barriers on the border, did just this.

A look at the change in the way executive orders have been used throughout history still brings uneasiness. The first 17 presidents each signed fewer than eighty executive orders, with most signing far fewer than that. In the entirety of George Washington's presidency, he signed only eight executive orders according to The American Presidency Project. In the first week of Trump's presidency, he signed seven. A comparison between the executive orders of the first and second halves of American presidents has shown just how much their role has expanded in American politics throughout history. George W. Bush penned 291 orders and Barack Obama, 276. This is nowhere near the record of 3,721 signed by Franklin D. Roosevelt.

With such a high number of executive orders, sometimes the line between an order that creates a new law and an order that utilizes existing laws is not always clear. Take for instance, Franklin D. Roosevelt's Executive Order 9066, which imprisoned hundreds of thousands of Japanese-Americans in one of the most controversial decisions of American history. If one man can make the decision to unjustly imprison hundreds of thousands of American citizens through executive order, it becomes clear that executive order grants the president far more power than interpreting and enforcing existing laws. The power to revoke legal residency and visas without any justification or legislative approval whatsoever has also now gone beyond just enforcing existing laws.

While the power granted by them is unsettling, executive orders have also shaped US history. Both the Louisiana Purchase and the Emancipation Proclamation were a result of executive orders from Thomas Jefferson and Abraham Lincoln, respectively. More recently, the Deferred Action for Childhood Arrivals has granted amnesty to hundreds of thousands of immigrants who have called America home since childhood. Executive orders can be used for good but their potential for destruction is large enough (as we saw with Roosevelt and are now seeing with Trump) that we should not let them go unchecked; there must be some limit placed on them.

With over 14,000 executive orders signed into action, it's clear that whether or not we like it, executive orders have been a major part of American history. With President Trump, Americans are now being awakened to the possible negativities of granting such power to one individual. With both the executive and legislative branches being controlled by the same party, the potential power that Trump could have through if executive orders are left unchecked is troubling. However, as we saw with a federal judge's order to halt Trump's immigration policy for visa holders, there is a limit on executive orders and as long as we remain cautious and wary of the possibilities, we can prevent the next generation of American internment camps.

Organizations to Contact

The editors have compiled the following list of organizations concerned with the issues debated in this book. The descriptions are derived from materials provided by the organizations. All have publications or information available for interested readers. This list was compiled on the date of publication of the present volume; the information provided here may change. Be aware that many organizations take several weeks or longer to respond to inquiries, so allow as much time as possible.

American Civil Liberties Union (ACLU)
125 Broad Street, 18th Floor
New York, NY 10004
(212) 549-2500
email: via website
website: www.aclu.org

The ACLU is a national organization that works daily in courts, legislatures, and communities to defend the individual rights and liberties guaranteed by the Constitution and laws of the United States.

American Constitution Society for Law and Policy (ACS)
1333 H Street NW, 11th Floor
Washington, DC 20005
(202) 393-6181
email: info@ACSLaw.org
website: www.acslaw.org

The ACS works for positive change by shaping debate on vitally important legal and constitutional issues through development and promotion of high-impact ideas to opinion leaders and the media; by building networks of lawyers, law students, judges and policymakers dedicated to those ideas; and by countering the activist conservative legal movement.

The American Council of Young Political Leaders (ACYPL)

1030 15th Street NW
Suite 580 West
Washington, DC 20005
(202) 857-0999
website: http://acypl.org

The ACYPL is a nonpartisan nonprofit organization that seeks to introduce future political and policy leaders to international affairs. It promotes mutual understanding and respect through establishing programs with strategically important countries, nascent democracies, and longtime allies, facilitating exchange programs with these countries. It also conducts multinational programs on topics of global or regional importance. Since its founding, ACYPL has worked in 121 countries.

American Political Science Association

1527 New Hampshire Avenue NW
Washington, DC 20036-1206
(202) 483-2512
email: apsa@apsanet.org
website: www.apsanet.org

The American Political Science Association is a professional association of political science students and scholars in the United States. Founded in 1903, it publishes three academic journals.

The Brennan Center for Justice
120 Broadway
Suite 1750
New York, NY 10271
(646) 292-8310
email: brennancenter@nyu.edu
website: www.brennancenter.org

The Brennan Center for Justice at NYU School of Law is a nonpartisan law and policy institute that pushes for transparency and justice in our political system. It works to hold political institutions and laws accountable for upholding the ideals of democracy through fighting for Constitutional protection in Congress, state legislatures, and the courts.

Cato Institute
1000 Massachusetts Avenue NW
Washington, DC 20001-5403
(202) 842-0200
website: www.cato.org

The Cato Institute is an American libertarian think tank headquartered in Washington, DC. Its mission is to promote an American public policy based on individual liberty, limited government, free markets, and peaceful international relations.

Center for Constitutional Rights
666 Broadway
7th Floor
New York, NY 10012
(212) 614-6464
website: www.ccrjustice.org

The Center for Constitutional Rights is dedicated to advancing and protecting the rights guaranteed by the US Constitution and the Universal Declaration of Human Rights.

The Constitution Project
1200 18th Street NW, Suite 1000
Washington, DC 20036
(202) 580-6920
email: info@constitutionproject.org
website: www.constitutionproject.org

The Constitution Project is a nonprofit think tank in the United States whose goal is to build bipartisan consensus on significant constitutional and legal questions.

Northeastern Political Science Association (NPSA)
86 Pine Street
Frostburg, MD 20153
(888) 479-0114
website: www.northeasternpsa.com

The NPSA is one the leading regional professional organizations in the United States for the study of politics.

Southern Political Science Association
Dept. of Political Science
Georgia State University
38 Peachtree Center Avenue
Atlanta, GA 30303-2514
(912) 739-2240
email: info@spsa.net
website: www.spsa.net

The Southern Political Science Association is one of the oldest and largest political science organizations in the United States. Founded in 1929, its primary purposes are to publish a professional journal, to promote interest and research in theoretical and practical political problems, and to encourage communication and respect between persons engaged in the professional study and practice of government and politics.

Teen Age Republicans
National TAR Headquarters
PO Box 2128
Manassas, VA 20108
(703) 368-4220
email: Info@TeenAgeRepublicans.org
website: www.teenagerepublicans.org

Teen Age Republicans is the national youth organization of the US Republican Party. Its aim is to provide support to the party and its candidates.

Young Democrats of America
PO Box 77496
Washington, DC 20013-8496
email: info@yda.org
website: www.yda.org

The Young Democrats of America has been the official youth arm of the Democratic Party since its founding in 1932. It has over 150,000 members nationwide, with chapters in 48 states and US territories—including high-school and college students, young workers, young professionals, and young families.

Bibliography

Books

Michelle Belco and Brandon Rottinghaus, *The Dual Executive: Unilateral Orders in a Separated and Shared Power System (Studies in the Modern Presidency)*. Palo Alto, CA: Stanford University Press, 2017.

Phillip Cooper, *By Order of the President: The Use and Abuse of Executive Direct Action (Studies in Government and Public Policy)*, 2nd edition. Lawrence: University of Kansas Press, 2014.

Louis Fisher, *Constitutional Conflicts between Congress and the President*, 6th edition. Lawrence: University of Kansas Press, 2014.

Daniel P. Gitterman, *Calling the Shots: The President, Executive Orders, and Public Policy*. Washington, DC: Brookings Institution Press, 2014.

David M. Konisky, *Failed Promises: Evaluating the Federal Government's Response to Environmental Justice (American and Comparative Environmental Policy)*. Cambridge, MA: MIT Press, 2015.

Michael Nelson, ed. *The Presidency and the Political System*, 10th edition. Washington, DC: CQ Press, 2013.

Joseph A. Pika and John Anthony Maltese, *The Politics of the Presidency*, revised 8th edition. Washington, DC: CQ Press, 2013.

Charlie Savage, *Power Wars: The Relentless Rise of Presidential Authority and Secrecy*. Boston, MA: Back Bay Books, 2017.

Barbara Sinclair, *Unorthodox Lawmaking: New Legislative Processes in the U.S. Congress*, 5th edition. Washington, DC: CQ Press, 2016.

Jeremy Suri, *The Impossible Presidency: The Rise and Fall of America's Highest Office.* New York, NY: Basic Books, 2017.

Periodicals and Internet Sources

Elizabeth B. Bazan, Johnny Killian, and Kenneth R. Thomas, "Congressional Authority Over the Federal Courts," Congressional Research Service, May 16, 2005. https://fas .org/sgp/crs/misc/RL32926.pdf.

Environmental Law Institute, "Regulatory Reform in the Trump Era," March 2017. https://www.eenews.net /assets/2017/03/24/document_gw_02.pdf.

Natasha Geiling, "Trump Just Gutted U.S. Policies to Fight Climate Change," Think Progress, March 28, 2017. https:// thinkprogress.org/trump-climate-change-clean-power -plan-climate-executive-order-2e162d4e7da1.

Rebecca Harrington, "Trump Signed 90 Executive Actions in His First 100 Days—Here's What Each One Does," *Business Insider*, May 3, 2017. http://www.businessinsider.com /trump-executive-orders-memorandum-proclamations -presidential-action-guide-2017-1/#executive-order-april -29-renegotiating-trade-agreements-1.

National Constitution Center Staff, "Executive Orders 101: What Are They and How Do Presidents Use Them?" National Constitution Center, January 23, 2017. https:// constitutioncenter.org/blog/executive-orders-101-what-are -they-and-how-do-presidents-use-them.

National Constitution Center Staff, "President Obama's Use of Executive Orders in Historical Terms," National Constitution Center, August 5, 2014. https:// constitutioncenter.org/blog/president-obamas-use-of -executive-orders-in-historical-terms.

National Public Radio, "Trump's Executive Order on Immigration, Annotated," January 31, 2017. https://www .npr.org/2017/01/31/512439121/trumps-executive-order -on-immigration-annotated.

Erica Newland, "Executive Orders in Court," *Yale Law Journal*, 2015. https://www.yalelawjournal.org/pdf/d.2026 .Newland.2099_xocajdzh.pdf.

John Woolley and Gerhard Peters, "Executive Orders: Washington—Trump," American Presidency Project, accessed December 28, 2017. http://www.presidency.ucsb .edu/data/orders.php.

Adam S. Zimmerman, "Presidential Settlements," *University of Pennsylvania Law Review* 163, June 16, 2010. http:// scholarship.law.upenn.edu/cgi/viewcontent .cgi?article=9481&context=penn_law_review.

Index